The Royal Wedding

FOR

DUMMIES®

The Royal Wedding

FOR

DUMMIES®

by Julian Knight

A John Wiley and Sons, Ltd, Publication

The Royal Wedding For Dummies®

Published by
John Wiley & Sons, Ltd
The Atrium
Southern Gate
Chichester
West Sussex
PO19 8SQ
England

Email (for orders and customer service enquires): cs-books@wiley.co.uk

Visit our Home Page on www.wiley.com

ISBN: 978-1-119-97030-9 (pbk), 978-1-119-97303-4 (ebk), 978-1-119-97304-1 (ebk), 978-1-119-97305-8 (ebk)

Printed and bound in Great Britain by TJ International

10 9 8 7 6 5 4 3 2 1

WILEY

About the Author

Julian Knight was born in 1972 in Chester. He was educated at the Chester Catholic High School and later Hull University, where he obtained a degree in History.

Julian has been a journalist since 1998 and has written for the *Guardian*, Financial Times Group and many other publications.

From 2002 to 2007 he was the personal finance and consumer affairs reporter for BBC News. Since 2007 he has been the Money and Property editor of the *Independent on Sunday* and has won many industry awards for his journalism. He has also authored *Wills, Probate, and Inheritance Tax For Dummies*, *Retiring Wealthy For Dummies*, *The British Citizenship Test For Dummies* and *Cricket For Dummies*.

Dedication

To Pip. Enjoy the big day! With all my love.

Publisher's Acknowledgments

We're proud of this book; please send us your comments through our Dummies online registration form located at www.dummies.com/register/.

Some of the people who helped bring this book to market include the following:

Acquisitions, Editorial and Media Development

Commissioning Editor: Mike Baker

Project Editor: Rachael Chilvers

Production Manager: Daniel Mersey

Assistant Editor: Ben Kemble

Proofreader: Andy Finch

Cartoons: Rich Tennant, www.the5thwave.com

Cover Photo: © Getty Images

Composition Services

Project Coordinator: Kristie Rees

Layout and Graphics: SDJumper, Corrie Socolovitch

Proofreader: Laura Albert

Indexer: Claudia Bourbeau

Publishing and Editorial for Consumer Dummies

Diane Graves Steele, Vice President and Publisher, Consumer Dummies

Kristin Ferguson-Wagstaffe, Product Development Director, Consumer Dummies

Ensley Eikenburg, Associate Publisher, Travel

Kelly Regan, Editorial Director, Travel

Publishing for Technology Dummies

Andy Cummings, Vice President and Publisher, Dummies Technology/General User

Composition Services

Debbie Stailey, Director of Composition Services

Contents at a Glance

Table of Contents

Introduction

● ●

*T*he royal wedding is, by far, the biggest British national celebration of 2011. Millions of people plan to watch on television as the energetic and dashing young Prince William and the beautiful Catherine (Kate) Middleton are married, and hundreds of thousands of well-wishers are expected to line the streets of London.

This book is designed to help you get the most from the build-up to the wedding event of the year and during the big day itself.

I cover everything you need to know about the participants and the wedding and how to organise your own festivities, from a street party to a fun quiz for friends and family.

William and Kate's wedding is the good news event of the year and this book shows you how to enjoy it to the max – happy reading!

About This Book

For Dummies books are all about giving you useful advice and information in a light easy-to-access format, and this one's no different. I go through the background to the royal wedding as well as royal weddings and major celebrations of the past. In addition, I look at the wedding itself, the venue and how best to view the whole event.

If you're visiting London I advise on where to stay and if you're staying at home how to organise your own celebrations and get the most from what's sure to be a day to remember.

This book is chock-full of hints and tips to help make life as easy as possible for you on the big day. What's more, the wedding's covered with a fair smattering of humour; the day's going to be fun and I hope this book is as well.

Conventions Used in This Book

To help you navigate through this book, I use a few conventions:

- ✔ *Italic* is used to highlight new words or terms that are defined.

- ✔ **Boldfaced** text is used to indicate the action part of numbered steps.

- ✔ Monofont is used for website addresses.

What You're Not to Read

I've written this book so that you can:

- ✔ Find relevant information easily.

- ✔ Understand easily what you find.

Although I'm sure that you want to pore over every last word between the two yellow covers, I identify material that you can skip if you so desire by placing such text in sidebars.

These sidebars share observations and interesting snippets, but although interesting and related to the topic in hand, this material isn't crucial or essential to know.

Foolish Assumptions

I make some general assumptions about you as follows:

- ✔ You aren't an expert on the royal family but want to know more.

- ✔ You're looking forward to the royal wedding day and want to consider all the options for having fun.

- ✔ You plan to watch the royal wedding at home on television or travel to London for the event.

If after reading this book you want to discover more about the royal family and its huge role in British history, check out *The British Monarchy For Dummies* by Philip Wilkinson or *British History For Dummies* by Sean Lang (both published by Wiley).

How This Book Is Organised

The Royal Wedding For Dummies is organised into four parts. The chapters within each part cover specific topic areas in more detail, so that you can easily and quickly find the topic you need.

Part 1: The Background

The chapters in this part give you background to the big day, and a rundown of the developing relationship between William and Kate. I take you into the inner sanctum of the royal family, giving you the lowdown on famous people who you normally see only on stamps or on the TV (in Chapters 1 and 2). In Chapter 3, I take you through some royal weddings of the past – the successful and less successful. Read Part I to get clued up on all things royal!

Part II: The Wedding

In this part I peer behind the scenes of the big day itself. In Chapter 4, I examine the venue (the gothic masterpiece Westminster Abbey), its history and describe some highlights for visitors, as well as look at what happens during the ceremony. Chapter 5 lifts the lid on the arcane world of royal etiquette – for example, what you should say if you bump into the Queen (the big clue is not to call her Liz). I also let you in on the wedding guest list, describing some famous faces you can spot among the guests in Chapter 6.

Part III: Taking Part in the Festivities

Part III is for you whether you're staying at home or travelling to London for the wedding day. Chapter 7 advises you on how to travel to the ceremony and what other sites to see while in one of the most exciting cities on earth.

If you decide to stay at home, I help you to organise a street party successfully and safely in Chapter 8. What's more, those looking to cook a celebratory meal are sure to eat up Chapter 9 on traditional British party fayre. If you

want to test your royal knowledge, check out how to set
up your own pub quiz in Chapter 10, which also provides
100 regal questions to challenge you and your friends.

Part IV: The Part of Tens

The famous Part of Tens is, of course, essential to any *For
Dummies* book. Chapters 11 and 12 contain ten websites
with must-know facts about the royals and the big day
and some royal palaces the newly-weds may stay at.

Icons Used in This Book

The small graphics in the margins of this book point to
specific bits of text that are worth focusing on.

As comedian Ben Elton used to say: 'Oh, a bit controversial that!'. Under this icon I describe some controversial
issues (for example, the civil list) or behaviour (Prince
Philip's not so occasional gaffes) that are bound to stir
up debate.

This icon contains useful and interesting nuggets to
expand your knowledge about all things royal-wedding
related.

Taking the information under this icon to heart helps you
get more from the royal wedding.

This icon indicates helpful pieces of information, so that
you can get the most from the day and even save some
time or money.

Where to Go from Here

As with all *For Dummies* books, the chapters in *The Royal Wedding For Dummies* are self-contained. In this way you can choose your own course through the book depending on your specific interests. For example, if your primary concern is what to do on the actual day, flip straight to Part III. If, on the other hand, you want to investigate the history of royal weddings or discover all about the magnificent setting (Westminster Abbey), check out Chapters 2 and 4 first.

The choice is yours. Whatever way you choose to use it, I hope that you enjoy this book and it adds to your enjoyment of the whole royal wedding experience.

Part I
The Background

The 5th Wave   By Rich Tennant

'I could rent you this one. It's got a pool in the backyard. Then I've got a six bedroom with a fountain out front, but nothing right now with a moat.'

In this part . . .

*T*he chapters in this part give you the background to the big day. I trace the history of the developing relationship between William and Catherine (Kate). I introduce you to the royal family and the Middletons, and we take a trip through time to attend royal weddings from the past.

Chapter 1

Charting the Course of the Royal Romance

'They've been practising for a long time,' was Prince Charles's laconic comment when Prince William and Catherine (Kate) Middleton announced their engagement to a delighted nation.

From meeting at university, sharing the same digs, supporting each other on entering the world of work and via a thankfully-temporary and amicable break-up, the relationship of Wills and Kate has been every inch a modern romance.

Now, at 11 a.m. on 29 April 2011, this on-off-on-again romance culminates in a national celebration; a wedding day to tell your grandchildren about.

But how did they (and the nation) get to this point? What ups and downs did the couple go through to arrive at a position where Kate said 'I do' to her dream prince?

In this chapter, I chart the relationship of William and Kate, the first great royal romance of the 21st century.

Living Life to the Full: University Days

Prince William's choice of the University of St Andrews in Scotland as a place to study was a major surprise. Not because St Andrews isn't a great university – it's one of the world's oldest and most respected – but because recent royals preferred the very formal colleges of Oxford and Cambridge.

By choosing St Andrews, William was perhaps marking out that he's slightly different from the older generation of royals and wants a more normal life.

Whatever his reasons, the choice was a wise one. He met the glamorous Kate Middleton, the eldest daughter of millionaire business couple Michael and Carole (I talk more about the Middleton family in Chapter 2).

Kate choosing to go to St Andrews seemed natural. After all, as a young child she was educated at a school with the same name: St Andrew's in the leafy village of Pangbourne in Berkshire.

So when did Wills and Kate first meet? Was it in the student union bar or at a dinner party with friends? Or perhaps their eyes locked on the narrow historic streets of St Andrews?

The real answer is, in fact, more glam. The story goes that William attended a charity fashion show in 2001 in which young Kate was one of the models. He paid £200 for a front-row seat, which turned out to be the best investment of his life!

The young Prince was smitten by Kate's undoubted good looks and by hook or by crook he managed to secure the all important first date! However, it took some time because they didn't start dating until around 2003. By then though, they were living under the same roof sharing university accommodation.

As for how their romance developed at university, however, the details are patchy and pervaded by an air of mystery.

Good reasons exist for the mystery, including:

- ✔ **Press ban:** The British press agreed to leave Prince William in peace during his time at school and university. This ban on coverage may be seen as a direct response to the death of William's mother Diana, who had been the subject of highly-intrusive media speculation (read more about Charles and Diana's relationship in Chapter 3).

- ✔ **Good friends:** Wills and Kate chose their university friends wisely, avoiding any hangers-on who looked to spread tittle-tattle or make a quick buck out of their association with the young couple.

The public first became aware of a potential royal romance when the pair were photographed on a ski holiday to Prince Charles's favourite Alpine resort of Klosters in March 2004.

Kate studied History of Art at university while Prince William studied the same before switching to Geography; both got a very creditworthy 2:1 degree.

Feeling the Pressure: Press Intrusion

Turning 21 is a big day for anyone, but particularly for William because it was in effect the young Prince's coming out party for the world's media.

The press's long-standing agreement to leave the Prince and his private life alone came to an end and suddenly the gloves were off.

Fortunately, William handles himself exceptionally well and seems very level-headed. Therefore, any sections of the press that loved dishing the dirt weren't able to because, frankly, no dirt was available to dish.

This fact, however, didn't stop the press taking a very keen interest in William's private life and his blossoming relationship with Kate Middleton. In addition, Kate's family – and in particular her younger sister Pippa – became the focus of intense media scrutiny. Again though, the Middletons generally kept themselves to themselves, and the press found little to say (which may not, perhaps, have been the case with all families!).

Regardless, William and Catherine were now playing a whole new game with the gossip columnists and paparazzi in overdrive. Yet they kept their dignity, and Kate's unwillingness to give public interviews meant that, despite being very much in public view, the relationship remained fairly private.

What's more, experts at Buckingham Palace provided excellent media-handling advice and the couple have been supported by a network of loyal friends who keep their confidences.

Like many couples William and Kate have nicknames for one another. Apparently Wills calls Kate 'Babykins' while she refers to the future king as 'Big Willie' . . . about which, enough said!

Moving into the World of Work

Many successful long-term couples say that the secret of their enduring romance is not being together 24 hours a day, every day, and to pursue their own interests and careers.

Royal watchers suspect that this is the secret to Wills and Kate's partnership. They share an interest in sport, the countryside, music and family, but they also have their own time and careers.

Kate worked in the past as retail buyer for clothing chain Jigsaw, but also found time to be supportive of Wills in his career.

William is a bit of high flyer . . . literally! He attended the Royal Military Academy at Sandhurst after university and became a lieutenant in the Army. Later, he transferred to the RAF where he became a flight lieutenant and ultimately a search-and-rescue pilot.

In October 2010, William attended his first rescue call as a co-pilot and is going to continue in the role as a pilot until 2013, with a break for his honeymoon of course!

No doubt all you romantics remember the film *An Officer and a Gentleman* in which Richard Gere's character turns up at the factory in his white US Navy uniform and carries off Debra Winger? Well, Wills isn't adverse to a bit of work-based romance, too. On one occasion he surprised Kate and her family at home by landing his search-and-rescue helicopter on the family lawn and popping in for tea – how dashing!

Hitting the Buffers: The Break-Up

In *A Midsummer Night's Dream* (Act I, Scene I), Shakespeare writes that 'The course of true love never did run smooth', and this statement certainly seems to relate to the romance of Wills and Kate.

The couple split officially in 2007. The pressures of intense media scrutiny were cited as a reason, but William also seems to have been not quite ready to settle down.

In 2005, William was reported as saying that he wouldn't marry until he was 28 or 30 years old! He proved to be right (he's 28)!

Kate was said to be devastated by the split from her prince, but again she kept a dignified silence, although her upset was reported to the press by some 'friends'.

But Kate didn't have to be upset for long, because reconciliation was soon on the cards. Within a few months she was attending royal family get-togethers and was again Prince William's girlfriend. Obviously the young Prince had seen the good sense to realise that he couldn't let her get away.

Moving into the Home Stretch: The Reconciliation

Rumours that Wills and Kate were back together again started almost from the moment that news of their break-up hit the newsstands in April 2007.

But just a couple of months later Kate attended the Concert for Diana at Wembley Stadium with Prince William; then in August they went on holiday together to Desroches Island in the Seychelles.

By June 2008 Wills and Kate were most definitely an item again when she attended William's investiture into the Order of the Garter, along with her future in laws, the Windsors (flip to Chapter 2 for all about the royal family, past and present).

This time around the relationship displayed a new seriousness, as if the couple had looked at what life would be like apart and decided that it wasn't for them.

Some journalists unkindly nicknamed Kate 'Waity' Katy during the course of the royal romance, not as a cruel jibe at her figure – which is worthy of a top model – but because she had to wait a long time for William to pop the question.

When Kate Middleton attended William's passing out parade at Sandhurst, the royal rumour mill went into overdrive. Royal watchers and columnists speculated that an engagement was on the cards. One retail chain, Woolworths, even went as far as to start selling royal wedding memorabilia – this was a false alarm and Woolworths even went bust a couple of years later.

Kate has a strong friendship with William's younger brother Harry. After the announcement of their engagement, Harry was quoted in the German press as saying, 'I always wished for a sister and now I have one.'

Popping the Question: The Engagement

Anyone who's dropped to one knee and proposed knows that how you pop the question is crucial. Planning pays dividends if you're to elicit the answer 'yes'!

William chose one of his favourite spots – the Lewa game reserve in Kenya – to ask Kate for her hand. The words he spoke are private but you can picture the scene . . .

William underlined his love by presenting Kate with his mother's engagement ring, inset with a stunning 18-carat sapphire. She said yes and the engagement was announced on their return from holiday.

Now Britain is geared-up to celebrate a glamorous royal wedding on 29 April 2011 – a very modern couple tying the knot in the traditional setting of Westminster Abbey. I take you on a tour of this marvellous building in Chapter 4 and provide info on some other royal palaces in Chapter 12.

If you plan to attend the procession and other celebrations in person, discover how to navigate your way around London on the big day in Chapter 7.

For loads of other ways in which you can play a part in the celebrations, check out Part III of this book: Chapter 8 for arranging a street party, Chapter 9 for the all-important guide to your own royal feast and Chapter 10 for how to organise a royal pub quiz.

Chapter 2

Gazing at the Royal Family

● ●

In This Chapter

▶ Discovering the Queen's ancestors

▶ Coming up to date with the Windsors

▶ Focusing on the families involved in the wedding

▶ Understanding Princess Diana's legacy

● ●

They're bigger than the Ewings from the 1980s hit US TV series *Dallas*. They're bigger than the Kennedys. And yes, they're even bigger than the Mitchells from *Eastenders*. The British royal family, otherwise known as the Windsors, is quite simply the most famous family in the world, bar none.

The right royal soap opera has been running for a millennium and yet people around the globe aren't tiring of the pomp, circumstance and even the occasional scandal.

In this chapter I peer behind all the pageantry to get at the roots of the modern royal family. I also introduce you to the Middletons, who are just about to join one of the greatest shows on earth.

So read on, and really get to know the royals.

Looking at the Queen's Ancestors

How far back can you trace your family tree?

Three generations, four, maybe five? If you check out *Researching Your Family History Online For Dummies* by Dr Nick Barratt and friends (Wiley) you may well be able to trace your ancestors back quite some way, but I bet nowhere near as long ago as the royals.

They can go back a thousand years or more through the ages with no problem. In fact, at one time many British schoolchildren could recite the names and dates of all the many kings and queens of England by heart, going back to the Norman Conquest in 1066. Much of British history was written through the prism of monarchy, and historians debated whether he or she was a good king or queen and why this battle was lost or won.

Until relatively recently, the history of Britain was essentially a history of the monarchy, dominated by these super powerful figures making policy and fighting (and sometimes losing) wars.

The Norman Conquest – in which William Duke of Normandy landed on the south coast of England and defeated the incumbent King Harold at the Battle of Hastings – is seen as the starting point for studying British and royal history.

Noting a few notables

William the Conqueror started up a line of kings and queens which runs to this day and Queen Elizabeth II.

Some of the current Queen's other notable ancestors include:

- **King Henry II (reigned 1154–1189):** He set up the court system and drew up many laws that still govern British lives today. Henry was a great reforming monarch.

- **King Henry VIII (reigned 1509–1547):** He dissolved the monasteries and broke away from the Roman Catholic Church to set up the Church of England. His descendant Queen Elizabeth II still sits at the top of the Church.

- **Queen Elizabeth I (reigned 1558–1603):** She fought off the invading Spanish Armada in 1588 and brought peace with Scotland, which in turn ultimately led to the Act of Union from which Great Britain was formed in 1707.

- **Queen Victoria (reigned 1837–1901):** She was such a success that Victoria had a whole era named after her – the Victorian Age. During Victoria's reign, Britain became a world superpower with a massive empire covering a quarter of the world's land surface. But Victoria didn't accomplish this by chopping people's heads off (like many predecessors) or leading armies. No, Victoria was a *constitutional monarch*, which means that she obeyed the leading politicians in Parliament and governed the country democratically.

Queen Elizabeth II is also a constitutional monarch and her role is largely ceremonial. She assiduously avoids the rough and tumble of politics and looks simply to follow the advice of the elected government and represent the interest of the UK at home and abroad.

Identifying some black sheep

Like any family, a fair share of black sheep and frankly rather useless members lurk in the past of the British royals. For the sake of balance, here are the worst of the Queen's ancestors, most of whom met a sticky end:

- ✔ **King John (reigned 1199–1216):** While his elder brother was away on the Crusades and being imprisoned in Europe, King John went about annoying his own barons and losing wars with France. Highly ineffectual and, as it turned out, not long for this world!

- ✔ **King Edward II (reigned 1307–1327):** Nestled between two highly successful kings, Edward I and Edward III, came Edward II who was, putting it mildly, a bit useless. He lost wars against France and Scotland (not part of the UK at the time) and was eventually deposed and killed while in Pontefract Castle, supposedly with a red hot poker – ouch!

- ✔ **King Charles I (reigned 1625–1649):** Regularly tops the list of the worst kings of all time. Fought and lost not one but two civil wars against his own Parliament, and was put on trial and beheaded – ouch again!

- ✔ **King George III (reigned 1760–1820):** Not his fault, but a mental illness meant that for much of his 60-year reign, George was locked up for his own good. But when he was let out and ruled his government, he managed to lose the American colonies – not a smart play!

Moving into Modern Times: The Windsors

The British royal family may be an ancient institution but the current group – the House of Windsor – is relatively modern.

A Windsor has been sitting on the throne since 1917. In that year, Britain was locked in a huge and bloody war with Germany and the British royal family had a bit of a problem – they had a lot of German ancestors.

The monarch at the time, George V, was the grandson of Queen Victoria and Prince Albert – and Albert was a German prince with the family name of Saxe-Coburg Gotha, a very, very German name.

As a result King George chose to change the family name – as did a lot of more humble German immigrants – in his case to Windsor after the castle in which the family lived (check out Chapter 12 for more on this grand family home).

Hence we have the House of Windsor today – the family into which Kate Middleton has chosen to marry.

Over the centuries, many families have sat on the English and later the British throne, including the Plantagenets, the Tudors and the Stuarts. One family would have the throne and then be deposed or die off naturally and the nearest relative – although with a different family name – took over. This eventuality is unlikely to befall the Windsors though; as the next section describes, an awful lot of them exist!

Queen Elizabeth has four children: Charles, Anne, Andrew and Edward. Charles is the Prince of Wales and next in line to the throne, while the other three also have their place in the pecking order. Although Anne, Andrew and Edward are unlikely to ever ascend to the throne, they still play a major role in the royal family, raising money and awareness for charity, championing their own and national causes as well as making public appearances.

Taking in the Personnel: The Windsors in Focus

At the last count, over 1,000 people are related to Queen Elizabeth II and, in theory at least, could ascend the throne if necessary. That's one massive family; just think of the Christmas get-togethers and all that catering!

Only a handful of these people, however, have any dealings with the Queen or the day-to-day running of the British monarchy.

This section provides a rundown of the movers and shakers in the royal family in order of their right to ascend the throne.

Although the process seems behind the times, the succession to the British throne operates on a 'boys first' principle. Put simply, even if the woman is older she always comes behind the man in the succession. So, for example, Princess Anne is the elder sister of Prince Edward, but Edward is ahead of her in the order of succession. I know it doesn't seem right but them's the rules although the succession act is now under review, so girls may be treated equally by the time Wills and Kate have children.

Calling in the A-Team: The Queen and Prince Philip

Her Majesty Queen Elizabeth II is the reigning monarch and so numero uno in the royal pecking order. She's the constitutional monarch with all the main duties that role entails.

The Queen has been on the throne since 1952 and all that time she's had Prince Philip, the Duke of Edinburgh, to support her as husband. You often see them together on engagements – giving speeches and meeting people; they're very much the royal A-Team. At the royal wedding, they'll be together to see their grandson William marry Kate.

Before he married Elizabeth, Prince Philip was a member of the Greek royal family and a very distant relative of the Queen. However, on marrying he gave up any claim to the Greek throne and threw in his lot with Queen Elizabeth and they've been a successful twosome ever since, looking after the best interests of the country.

Queen Elizabeth is a masterful public speaker who rarely puts a foot wrong. Prince Philip though . . . Well, how can I put it? He occasionally puts his foot right in it, with politically-incorrect utterances. Regardless of his foot-in-the-mouth tendency, he's a highly popular figure and someone who's seen as an example of true public service and a bit of a character.

Looking at the next in line: The Prince of Wales

Prince Charles cuts a controversial public figure compared to the Queen and Prince Philip – particularly after the painful divorce with William's mother Princess Diana (see the later section 'Understanding Diana's Legacy').

As the eldest son of the Queen, Charles is the next in line to the throne and all his offspring take precedent in the succession over his siblings and their children.

He has staunch and well-publicised views on farming, architecture and the environment and many see him as an intelligent and valued voice who uses his position to make points on matters of genuine importance. Some critics, though, suggest that he ought to steer clear of controversy because one day he's very likely to be King Charles III.

Prince Charles has used some of his money and his title as the Duke of Cornwall to promote the growing of organic food on his estate as well as the construction of a model architectural town called Poundbury in the county of Dorset.

Prince Charles remarried following the divorce and subsequent death of Princess Diana. The lady he chose was a long-standing friend and fellow countryside enthusiast Camilla, now the Duchess of Cornwall. And when Charles eventually ascends the throne, every possibility exists that the UK may have a Queen Camilla.

Adding a touch of glamour: Prince William and Kate Middleton

As Charles's eldest son and the Queen's grandson, William is third in line to the throne. So the British people are likely to see him as King William one day, alongside his university sweetheart and soon-to-be-wife Kate Middleton.

William has some of the same stardust as his mother Princess Diana. Good looking, easy to get along with and comfortable with the public, he's seen as every inch the modern prince who can take the monarchy well into the 21st century.

A trained search-and-rescue pilot and supporter of Aston Villa football club, William resonates well with the public and is a hugely popular figure. He's also passionate – like the other royals – about charitable work and isn't afraid to get his hands dirty on trips to Africa and South America in aid of the poor.

Kate in turn has proved a hit with the photographers and the public due to her elegance, poise and calm in public interviews. Many admire her for her steadfastness when the couple temporarily separated. The eventual engagement in 2010 lifted the mood of a nation that was suffering an economic recession. See the later section 'Peering at the Bride's Side: The Middletons' for more about the Middleton family.

Supporting his brother: Prince Harry

Prince Harry has found a fantastic career in the army. He's an accomplished soldier and leader, said to be both brave and unassuming by those who've served alongside him in trouble-spots around the globe.

As Charles's youngest son, Harry is currently fourth in line to the throne but will slip down the pecking order if William and Kate have children. He's seen as a strong-willed character who likes to go to nightclubs, play sports and let off steam from what must be a highly stressful job. As far as William and Harry go, sibling rivalry doesn't exist and they're firm friends.

Checking out Charles's siblings: Andrew, Anne and Edward

All three of Prince Charles's siblings are very different characters and well-known to the public. Here's a quick rundown of these major royals:

- ✔ **Prince Andrew, Duke of York:** A decorated helicopter pilot in the Falklands war, Andrew is currently an ambassador for British business and a mad-keen golfer. He travels the world making contacts and trying to bring investment and jobs to the UK.

- ✔ **Anne, Princess Royal:** A highly popular member of the royal family, a fine horsewoman and a worker for charity, Anne's noted for her intelligence and laconic wit. She has a strong association with Scotland and is very much a favourite royal among those north of the border.

- ✔ **Prince Edward, Earl of Wessex:** Edward seemed to struggle to find a role in public life for a time when he left marine training and then formed his own theatre production company. But Edward has taken like a natural to the hardest job of all – raising a family – and conducts many public engagements on behalf of the Queen and Prince Philip.

Both Prince Andrew and Princess Anne have divorced and, in Anne's case, remarried. Andrew married Sarah Ferguson and had two children with her (Beatrice and Eugenie, who are William and Harry's cousins), but they eventually drifted apart and divorced in 1996. However, they remain firm friends. Likewise, Anne divorced from Captain Mark Phillips in 1992 (they also have two children, Peter and Zara) and subsequently married Commander Timothy Laurence.

Funding the monarchy

By many accounts, Queen Elizabeth II is one of the richest people in the world, and yet UK taxpayers pay her millions of pounds a year to perform the role of monarch. This amount isn't a salary, however. Instead the monarch uses the money to perform her official duties – think of it as expenses for the valuable work Her Majesty does.

Queen Elizabeth also distributes part of this money to her family in order to help with their living expenses and the costs associated with carrying out official duties on her (and therefore) her subjects' behalf.

The civil list causes a certain amount of controversy but royal supporters say that the money is very well spent because of the extra tourism that a monarchy generates, as well as the valuable work the royal family does in promoting good causes and British business.

Prince Edward married Sophie Rhys-Jones in 1999, and they have two children, Louise and James. Edward will assume the title of Duke of Edinburgh, his father's current title, when it becomes vacant.

Widening the net: The minor royals

Loads of people have a connection to the royal family (and some gain notoriety as a result). None have any chance of ascending to the throne but they are royals and as such enjoy celeb status. Not all court publicity, however – in fact some positively shun it. Here are two of the lesser but still interesting stars in the royal universe:

  ✔ **Zara Phillips:** Princess Anne's daughter is a chip off the old block, a world-class equestrian who won the BBC Sports Personality of the Year award in 2006.

Her striking good looks make her a favourite in the newspapers but she's inherited much of her mother's common sense. She'll soon be marrying England rugby star Mike Tindall.

✔ **Lord Snowdon:** The royal family's favourite photographer and renowned worldwide for his abilities with the camera, Lord Snowdon, who was married to Princess Margaret (the Queen's sister), until 1978 made his name in the 1960s and has risen to prominence through genuine ability rather than simply his royal connections.

Peering at the Bride's Side: The Middletons

'It takes two to tango', as the saying goes, and the same number for a happy wedding day! The Windsors may have all the titles – not to mention the castles – but some interesting characters are going to populate Kate's side of the church as well.

Kate's parents, Michael and Carole, made their fortune from a mail-order company called Party Pieces which, as you can probably guess, sells party supplies.

The family of Kate's mum Carole consists of miners and labourers from County Durham in the north of England.

Despite only forming Party Pieces in 1987, the Middletons became millionaires – so they must be very canny business people – and rich enough to educate their daughter privately at the prestigious Marlborough College and then St Andrews University – where Kate met William and fell in love.

Kate's younger sister Pippa has attracted the interest of the press for her lifestyle and relationships.

Kate and William are related to each other, but before you start worrying, they're cousins 15 times removed! They have a common ancestor located way back in the 16th century, and a fair amount of water has passed under the bridge since then.

Understanding Diana's Legacy

In her lifetime, Princess Diana was one of the world's most famous women. On her engagement to Prince Charles, as a shy 20-year-old, she appeared to be the fairytale princess. Blushing and coy, she stunned the world with her wedding dress and poise at the ceremony.

But things soon went wrong for Charles and Di, and despite two healthy sons – William and Harry – their relationship became very stormy. Charles was accused of being cold to Diana and retaining a long-term liaison with the married Camilla Parker Bowles. Diana, on the other hand, threw herself into her charitable roles and captured the public imagination. She showed the human touch with her work with AIDS patients and the HALO Trust, increasing awareness about the terrible human cost of land mines in combat zones.

When they divorced, the split was nearly as public as their wedding, with each party giving TV interviews. The episode was a low moment for the monarchy and much of the public sided with Diana.

Diana, Princess of Wales as she became known after her divorce, embarked on some high profile romances. The final fateful one was with Dodi Fayed, the son of Harrod's owner Mohamed Al Fayed. The courting couple died tragically in a car accident in Paris in 1997.

The accident wasn't the end of the Diana story – the worldwide public grief shown at her death rocked the foundations of the monarchy and ensured that she maintains a unique place in British history. In fact, Diana came second in a 2000 vote to find the most important Briton of all time.

As you'd expect, the death of their mother profoundly affected William and Harry. But it also ensured a deep well of public affection for them, which will be glimpsed no doubt during the royal wedding between Kate and William.

In a lovely touch, when Kate accepted William's proposal, he presented her with the same blue sapphire engagement ring that his father had given to his mother. William said that this act was his way of ensuring that his mother was part of the happy day.

Chapter 3

Revisiting Royal Marriages of the Past

● ●

In This Chapter

▶ Asking why royals marry

▶ Discovering some historic royal marriages

▶ Peering into modern royal nuptials

▶ Shedding tears over some royal divorces

● ●

Most Britons love a good royal wedding: the pomp, the ceremony, the jaw-dropping dresses and uniforms. But royal weddings and marriages are about much more than that.

Royals aren't quite like us mere mortals – that's why they're royal after all! – they marry for all sorts of reasons and not only love.

In this chapter, I take a look at the royal weddings and marriages of the past, revealing the successes and failures.

For a bit fun, I even award points out of ten to each royal couple according to the success of their marriage. See whether you agree with my ratings.

Looking at Why Royals Wed

Ask most couples why they married and they probably answer 'for love', at least if asked in front of one another! But if you were able to climb in a time machine and ask the same question of the kings and queens of the past, you'd hear all sorts of different reasons.

You see, up until relatively recently, the British royal family wielded huge political power. The reigning monarch is the head of the Church of England and laws made in Parliament are passed and executed in the sovereign's name. The courts dispense justice in the name of the monarch and up until the late 17th century, monarchs were powerful enough to take the country to war if they wanted.

For most of the UK's history, the centre of political power has resided in the throne rather than Parliament. Therefore, royal marriages were a matter of politics, with unions made to advance the interest, power and wealth of the royal family as well as to safeguard the security of the country.

Here are some reasons why royal marriages used to take place:

- ✔ **Political alliances.** The idea was that a monarch wanted to form an alliance with a foreign country (often ruled by another royal family) and so would marry into that family themselves or instruct their son, daughter or other relative to do so. As a result, bride and groom often didn't meet until the wedding day, in what was, in effect, an arranged marriage.

✔ **To secure the succession.** Up until the 20th century, life was often very short, even for members of the royal family. Therefore they felt compelled to have children – particularly sons – in double-quick time so that they had someone to leave their throne to.

✔ **To end a war.** In the Middle Ages, it was a common ploy by monarchs to marry off a son, daughter or other relative to the family of someone with whom they wanted to sign a peace treaty. The idea was to show good faith and cement a new friendship. So, two monarchs who'd been fighting one another in battle only months before were able to stand happily beside each other giving a relative away in a church a few months later, and no one thought it unusual!

✔ **For love.** Yes it did happen. Sometimes a royal met someone and just had to marry, no matter what. And royals (such as King Edward VIII) even gave up the right to sit on the throne to marry the person they loved.

Arranged marriages often end with both partners loving one another. British royal history is littered with couples who met for the first time on their wedding day, but an intense bond grew between them.

Henry VIII, who reigned from 1509–1547, was an ancestor of the current Queen. Henry was very unlucky in marriage (though not as unlucky as his wives) and had six wives in a bid to have a son. He eventually got a son, Edward VI, but he only outlived his father by six years, dying as a teenager.

Delving into the Past: Royal Marriages

Britain has had a monarchy for over 1,000 years, making the royal family one of the great survivors of history. The success of individual monarchs, however, was often less to do with how many battles they won or how many laws they made but who they married and whether the marriage was a success or failure.

Looking back over the long span of history, here are some of the most and least successful royal marriage partnerships.

Henry II and Eleanor of Aquitaine

This union defied the conventions of its day. For starters, Eleanor was 12 years older than Henry, the future King of England. What's more, Eleanor had already been married and widowed and was reputed to have a brilliant, calculating mind. And get this: she was supposedly a former lover of Henry's father. In all, the story would make a great soap opera plot!

Even after Henry II ascended the English throne in 1154, his and Eleanor's relationship was one of equals – something that was highly unusual in the 12th century. Despite this, they fought like cat and dog and Henry even had Eleanor imprisoned on occasions. They were obviously not completely incompatible, however, because Eleanor fell pregnant eight times.

Henry proved to be a highly successful monarch but Eleanor outlived him. Their son Richard I was nicknamed the Lionheart.

For Dummies marriage success score:
An unconventional 6/10

Henry VII and Elizabeth of York

Victor of the Battle of Bosworth in 1485, Henry Tudor was crowned Henry VII. His claim to the throne was tenuous and many thought he wouldn't last long before being deposed. He needed friends fast and married Elizabeth of York, who was aligned with the Yorkist side in the War of the Roses – Henry was a Lancastrian.

This move was a masterstroke because it brought legitimacy to his rule and helped bring the War of the Roses, which had been raging for two decades, to an end. Elizabeth proved a wise queen and provided Henry with two sons – the youngest of which went on to be Henry VIII. When Elizabeth died, Henry VII was heartbroken but the country was at peace.

For Dummies marriage success score:
A politically masterful 9/10

Henry VIII and Anne Boleyn

All Henry VIII's six marriages were pretty eventful, but his second union to the charismatic Anne Boleyn is particularly notorious.

This marriage was very much lust-at-first-sight, with Henry being sweet on Anne. He also wanted a son very badly and his first marriage to Catherine of Aragon had little chance of providing one. So Henry divorced Catherine and in the process took England out of the Roman Catholic Church, forming the Church of England.

Violence and bloodshed followed and although he married Anne, she gave him a daughter rather than a son (the future Queen Elizabeth I) and he fell out of love with her. The marriage has a terrible postscript: Henry had Anne tried and executed for treason.

> **For Dummies marriage success score:**
> A disastrous 0/10

George IV and Caroline of Brunswick

George IV – or 'Georgy porgy' as he was nicknamed – was a heavy drinker and gambler. While Prince of Wales he ran up huge debts, which his father refused to honour until he married a woman of his choosing. Sadly, daddy chose badly in Caroline of Brunswick.

George and Caroline hated each other – it was loathe at first sight. Married in 1795 the two separated the following year although remained married. George, who ascended the throne in 1820, made attempts to have the marriage annulled – despite the fact that in their short time together they had a daughter – and even asked Parliament to investigate whether she was unfaithful.

All the time, George was carrying out a host of highly public affairs himself. His hypocrisy turned the public against him and in favour of Caroline.

> **For Dummies marriage success score:**
> An unloving 2/10

Queen Victoria and Prince Albert

This marriage was a love match tragically cut short. Young Queen Victoria married the dashing German Prince Albert in 1839 soon after she came to the throne. Belying the convention of the time she proposed to him!

The couple were deeply in love; Albert took the title Queen's Consort and became an invaluable source of advice. They managed the astounding feat of having nine children together and their family life was held up as an ideal in Victorian society. But behind the scenes all wasn't well, Albert was upset at the philandering behaviour of their eldest son Edward and as a result took on too many duties for the Queen; in short he made himself ill.

After a short bout of typhoid fever in 1861, Albert died and Victoria was heartbroken. Until her own death 40 years later Victoria always wore black and never forgave her son Edward for the worry he brought Albert.

> **For Dummies marriage success score:**
> A loyal and loving 9/10

Considering Some Modern Royal Couplings

The idea that a modern royal would marry in order to cement a political alliance or bring a war to an end is frankly daft. Although still a key thread of the UK's social fabric, royals are no longer big political players.

The modern, constitutional British monarch assiduously stays out of the murky world of politics, concentrating on civic duties and providing a moral example to the nation. For example, you never hear the Queen debating the rights and wrongs of tuition fees or whether the UK should join the Euro.

As a result, what royals look for in their ideal life partner has changed. They get to choose who they want to be with instead of having someone chosen for them.

In addition, they don't have to marry other royals – there aren't that many to go around in the 21st century. For example, Prince Edward, the Queen's youngest son, married Sophie Rhys-Jones who was a public relations executive, and Kate Middleton's family, although wealthy, aren't royal.

The royal marriage game has changed and this fact is represented in the more modern couplings of the past few decades. Here's a selection, for better or for worse, of some of the most interesting!

Queen Elizabeth II and the Duke of Edinburgh

This royal coupling is the epitome of 'for better or for worse'.

The Queen and the future Duke of Edinburgh met when he was asked to escort her and her younger sister Margaret on a tour of Dartmouth's Royal Naval College in 1939. The young Princess Elizabeth, as she was then called, was smitten with the dashing Philip.

The couple wrote to each other during the Second World War and in 1946 Philip asked for Elizabeth's hand in marriage. They've been a very successful partnership ever since.

The Queen ascended the throne in 1952 and Philip, by then the Duke of Edinburgh, has been steadfastly by her side during some tumultuous times for the royal family, particularly following the death of Princess Diana.

> **For Dummies marriage success score:**
> An unbeatably successful 10/10

Prince Charles and the Duchess of Cornwall

This union is Charles's second marriage and many people believe that it should have been his first. Like the Queen and Prince Philip's, the marriage is very much a love match with Charles and the Duchess, formerly Camilla Parker Bowles, sharing a keen interest in the environment, horses, hunting and shooting.

However, despite a long-standing liaison in early life, Charles and Camilla had to wait until late middle age to tie the knot because they were both married to other people – he to Princess Diana and she to Major Parker Bowles.

They've been wed for only a few years (since 9 April 2005) but their marriage can be judged a success in so far as much of the public antagonism that was felt towards Camilla following the death of Princess Diana has largely dissipated. (Diana famously said that three people were in her marriage to Charles – the third being Camilla.)

When Charles ascends the throne he may well do so with Camilla by his side as queen; just a few years ago the public mood would've made that highly unlikely.

> **Dummies marriage success score:**
> A long-delayed 6/10

Prince Edward and the Countess of Wessex

Prince Edward – the Earl of Wessex and youngest son of the Queen – spent a long time in his youth trying to find a role in society. He dropped out of intense training for the marines and had a short career in theatre production.

But since he met public relations executive Sophie Rhys-Jones and married in 1999, he's found a successful role as family man. Their wedding was less formal than those of Edward's siblings in that it was held in St George's Chapel at Windsor Castle. The Earl and Countess of Wessex, as they're now titled, have two children (Louise and James).

They have experienced problems – for instance, the media accused Edward and Sophie of making money from their position. In particular, Edward's production company produced a film about Prince William while he was studying at St Andrew's, allegedly against the wishes of some members of the royal family.

After relinquishing their interests in theatre and television, however, the couple's popularity within the royal family and in the country in general improved.

As any married person can tell you, getting on with the in-laws is important and Sophie certainly gets on with the Queen. They share a love of horses and a keen interest in military history, and are said to have a warm relationship.

> **Dummies marriage success score:**
> A like-minded 8/10

Princess Anne and Timothy Laurence

This marriage was the Princess Royal's second crack at nuptials, after marrying the dashing Captain Mark Phillips in 1973, only to divorce in 1992. Within six months of the divorce coming through Anne married again and to another military man, Commander in the Royal Navy Timothy Laurence – clearly she has a thing for men in uniforms!

The couple married in Scotland because the Church of England doesn't allow divorced people to get married in church. The ceremony was very low-key and not televised – unlike Charles's and Andrew's. The wedding indicated the couple's preference to stay out of the public eye – apart from when the Princess Royal is performing her royal engagements.

This approach seems to work with the public: in polls Anne emerges consistently as one of the most successful and popular royals.

> **Dummies marriage success score:**
> A second-time-round successful 9/10

Splashing the Cash: Lavish Royal Weddings

Royal weddings aren't just about the coming together of two people, hopefully for life. They're about a national celebration, British prestige and projecting to the world the continuing health of the monarchy. Many of the royal weddings of the past have been lavish affairs putting Posh and Becks or Russell Brand and Katy Perry to shame in the bling stakes.

But although the royals are rich and famous, they aren't here-today, gone-tomorrow celebrities (fortunately) and they're never naff: instead, they combine lavish with tasteful like no other family.

In these times of economic difficulty, though, a really lavish royal wedding can backfire. Princess Victoria, next in line to the Swedish throne, married her former personal trainer in June 2010. The ceremony and celebrations cost millions and brought Stockholm to a complete halt. Although 200,000 well-wishers clogged the streets of Stockholm, the event angered a hefty percentage of the population who thought that the wedding was over the top and too expensive.

In fact, 57,000 Facebook users joined an online protest against the wedding. A bit of a royal own-goal, then!

Royal weddings aren't all glitz, glamour and excess. When Elizabeth, the present Queen, married Prince Philip in 1947, their wedding, although full of pomp, was actually done on the cheap. The war had only just finished, Britain was broke and rationing was still in place. Elizabeth had to save up her rations for material to make the wedding dress just like any ordinary bride!

But back to the fun. This section describes some of the genuine bling-tastic UK royal wedding shindigs of the past.

King Henry VIII and Catherine of Aragon

The marriage of Henry to the first of his six wives was celebrated with lavish feasts, musical concerts and of course the obligatory jousts. Henry was a strapping lad at the time – before too many lavish feasts took their toll – and he took part in the jousting and general macho posturing, unsurprisingly beating all his opponents (who would think it a good career move to beat the King of England?).

Henry was seen as every inch the renaissance king – good at sports (brilliant at 'real' tennis apparently) and an intellectual to boot. Only later did he bloat out and start condemning his queens to death – Catherine was one of the lucky ones; he only divorced her!

Strangely, jousting to celebrate a royal wedding is set for a comeback. A tournament is due to take place at Blenheim Palace in Oxfordshire on 29 April 2011, to celebrate the nuptials of William and Kate.

Queen Victoria and Prince Albert Saxe-Coburg Gotha

As monarch of the most powerful country in the world, Victoria's wedding in February 1840 was a hugely important deal. Although 24-hour news channels didn't exist, the nation and the wider world was still enthralled by the young queen's marriage to the tall, handsome German prince.

The wedding, although relatively low-key compared to some royal weddings of the 1980s, was still seen as wildly extravagant particularly in the choice of dress.

Victoria chose to be married in a white dress made especially for the occasion and meant to be worn only the once. The dress went completely against convention, which was to have a more practical colour – even black – so that it could be worn time and again.

Prince Charles and Lady Diana Spencer

With its 8-metre (25-foot) long train, Diana's dress summed up what for many was the iconic royal wedding. Hundreds of thousands of people lined the streets and 20 million sat before their television sets in the UK to witness what seemed like a fairytale come true.

A staggering 3,500 guests attended the ceremony on 29 July 1981 at the giant St Paul's Cathedral; so many that 27 wedding cakes had to be made for the occasion. One estimate put the total cost of the wedding – including police and security – at a whopping £30 million, equivalent to £80 million in today's prices. But, despite the expense, things didn't go well for the couple (read more about the story in the later section 'Prince Charles and Princess Diana').

Who's paying for the wedding?

William and Kate's wedding is taking place at a time when Britain is recovering from the most severe recession since the Second World War. The country has massive debts and the government is making painful public spending cuts. Reflecting the tough economic times, a royal spokesperson has said that 'the wedding will be done properly and well but not in an ostentatious and lavish manner'.

Guest numbers are likely to be lower than for the marriage of William's parents Charles and Diana in 1981, with uncertainty over whether US president Barack Obama gets an invite (his presence would boost security costs massively).

The royal family is understood to be paying for the venue – Westminster Abbey – but this is only a fraction of the cost. The big expense is security and police and the final bill for the couple's happy day is expected to round £10 million.

What's more, the date of the wedding has been criticised – it falls on a Friday, a working day and just before a long bank holiday weekend. Business leaders have estimated the costs to the economy in lost production of having an extra public holiday on the day of a royal wedding at £5 billion! But I don't hear anyone else complaining . . .

Doing the Splits: Royal Divorce

The recent history of royal marriages hasn't been a happy one: three of the Queen's four children are divorced, though two have remarried happily. Even the Queen's now deceased sister Princess Margaret married and then divorced.

Doing the splits isn't a modern royal phenomenon – in the past many royals were married but eventually lived apart. In the current 24-hour news world and less deferential times, however, the public gets to hear about what's going on behind the palace doors.

As a result, relationships come under scrutiny as never before and most couples would struggle with the pressure of that. William and Kate can expect similar scrutiny but most observers agree that they're very well equipped to cope.

This section takes a look at some recent royal couplings that sadly fell by the wayside.

Prince Andrew and Sarah Ferguson, Duchess of York

The couple married in 1986 – in a ceremony nearly as lavish as the one five years earlier between Charles and Diana. Andrew and Sarah seemed to have a good chance of success because they were clearly a love match. On their wedding day they were given the titles of the Duke and Duchess of York and all seemed well. They went on to have two daughters Beatrice and Eugenie.

Tabloid stories soon emerged, however, of the Duchess's extravagant lifestyle and the couple's gradual estrangement.

They separated in 1992 and divorced in 1996 but managed to remain firm friends, speaking often on the phone and meeting socially, which is more grown up than many divorced couples behave!

Princess Margaret and Lord Snowdon

The Queen's sister was a major figure in swinging sixties London and is alleged to have enjoyed several romances with leading socialites of the time. But in 1960 she met and married well-known photographer Antony Armstrong-Jones.

The wedding of the glamorous pair was watched on television by 300 million viewers worldwide. Jones was created Lord Snowdon and all seemed well as they whizzed around London in their Mini to parties and show openings.

 Gradually the couple grew apart, however, and Margaret was rumoured (though never proved) to have had affairs with Peter Sellers and Mick Jagger.

Princess Margaret and Lord Snowdon divorced in 1978.

Princess Anne and Captain Mark Phillips

The story of Anne, Princess Royal and the dashing Captain Mark Phillips is nowhere near as sensational as her aunt Margaret splitting from Lord Snowdon. In many respects Anne's first marriage was fairly successful; they had two children, Peter and Zara Phillips (check out Chapter 2 for more on Zara), and preferred a quiet private life.

But as can happen, the couple started to drift apart and in 1989 they announced their intention to separate. The divorce was finalised in 1992.

Prince Charles and Princess Diana

This marriage was part soap opera, part fairytale and, sadly, part tragedy.

On marrying the beautiful Lady Diana Spencer in 1981 – who was aged just 20 – the Prince seemed to have secured the monarchy for a generation. The ceremony captured the imagination of the public in its lavish splendour and Princess Diana instantly became the most famous woman in the world. They had two children, Princes William and Harry, and all seemed superficially well.

In a book published in 1992, Prince Charles was alleged to have restarted his affair with former flame Camilla Parker Bowles.

Diana herself is believed to have formed attachments with men such as James Hewitt and James Gilbey during this difficult period of her marriage. Whatever the rights and wrongs of the situation the writing was on the wall for Charles and Diana and they divorced in 1996. Within a year, tragically, Diana was dead following a car crash in Paris and the nation mourned.

Edward and Mrs Simpson

The crisis that hit the monarchy after the death of Diana, Princess of Wales has only one recent parallel: the abdication crisis in 1936, and love was at the root of that.

King Edward VIII had just ascended the throne and he had a secret — his love for an American divorcee called Wallace Simpson. He wanted to make her his queen but politicians in Britain and in Commonwealth countries such as Australia and Canada said that the monarch marrying a divorcee was impossible.

In short, King Edward was given a choice: to give up the woman he loved or give up the throne. Edward chose the latter and he and Mrs Simpson, who did indeed marry, left Britain never to return.

Part II
The Wedding

'It's an electronic wedding planner. It'll create all your checklists and timetables, and after the ceremony it turns all the documents into confetti and throws it in your face.'

In this part . . .

Come with me and take a peek behind the scenes of the big day. Here I introduce you to Westminster Abbey – the grand stage for today's events and a building steeped in history. I also introduce the guests and provide you with some fun insight into the pageantry and etiquette on display.

Chapter 4

Taking a Tour of Westminster Abbey

· ·

In This Chapter

▶ Using the Abbey over the centuries

▶ Constructing the Abbey

▶ Touring the Abbey and its treasures

· ·

*W*estminster Abbey is no ordinary church; the ancient, magnificent building has been a major centre of royal and British life for 1,000 years, as well as the scene for loads of important events in British history – from coronations to royal weddings. In addition, the great and the good alike, such as kings, poets and scientists, are interred or memorialised in Westminster Abbey.

Now a new chapter is about to be written in the history of Westminster Abbey when Prince William and Kate Middleton get married there on 29 April 2011. The popular second-in-line to the throne (after his father, Prince Charles) and his beautiful bride are set to add a little sparkle to the sometimes sombre Abbey.

In this chapter I focus on the venue for William and Kate's wedding, as one of the great buildings of the Middle Ages hosts a very modern couple's wedding ceremony.

Understanding the Importance of Westminster Abbey

Located a stone's throw from the Houses of Parliament and a short walk from Buckingham Palace and 10 Downing Street – the residence of the Prime Minister – Westminster Abbey is quite literally at the centre of political and royal life in the UK.

Westminster Abbey is a massive building catering to hundreds of thousands of visitors each year; it's also a fully working church with its very own choir. The person who ensures that the magnificent building is kept in tip-top condition is the Dean of Westminster, who's appointed by the reigning monarch.

Plans call for the current Dean of Westminster, the Very Rev. John Hall, to play a prominent role on 29 April when he conducts the service. The Archbishop of Canterbury and the Bishop of London also have key roles to play; see Chapter 6 for details.

Over the centuries Westminster Abbey has become a touchstone for British public life. Here are just some of the important ceremonies that the Abbey hosts:

- ✓ Burials of very famous people, including kings and queens.
- ✓ Weddings of members of the royal family.
- ✓ Coronations of new monarchs.

What's in a name?

Westminster Abbey isn't called Westminster Abbey at all, no not a bit of it. Officially its name is the Collegiate Church of St Peter at Westminster, which is quite a mouthful. So over the years the building became popularly known as Westminster Abbey for the very good reason that it's slap bang in the middle of Westminster and was originally an abbey.

Technically speaking, today the Abbey is a 'Royal Peculiar', which means that it falls under the jurisdiction of the monarch and not a bishop or archbishop, although for a short period (1540–1550) it did have the status of a cathedral (Henry VIII wanted a reason for it to avoid the destruction that so many other abbeys suffered during this period).

Westminster Abbey was chosen for the climactic scene of Dan Brown's blockbuster novel *The Da Vinci Code.*

Laying the elite to rest

If you're really, really successful in life – and I don't mean simply make lots of money, become a TV star or even write the odd *For Dummies* guide – you may just be buried at Westminster Abbey.

Obviously you aren't going to be in any condition to appreciate the honour, but nevertheless your descendants will know that you were sufficiently important to the social or cultural life of the UK that the monarch of the day decided that you were worthy to be buried with Britain's greats.

As a guide to the illustrious company you'd be bedding down with for all eternity, here are some of those buried or having a permanent memorial at the Abbey:

- ✔ **Writers.** Geoffrey Chaucer, William Blake, Lord Byron, Charles Dickens, T.S. Eliot, the Bronte sisters and William Wordsworth.

  The area of Westminster Abbey where many of the nation's great writers are memorialised is called Poet's Corner.

- ✔ **Composers.** Henry Purcell, Vaughan Williams and Edward Elgar.

- ✔ **Politicians.** Clement Attlee, William Gladstone, William Pitt and his son William Pitt the younger.

- ✔ **Scientists.** Isaac Newton and Charles Darwin.

Add to this array copious numbers of royals, famous generals and politicians and you can see that the Abbey is more than a building; it's a celebration and commemoration of the past millennium of British life.

Although many of Britain's kings and queens are buried at Westminster Abbey, since George II (who died in 1760), the majority have been buried at St George's Chapel at Windsor Castle or the royal mausoleum at Frogmore House (check out Chapter 12 for more on the major royal palaces).

When the present Queen's mother Elizabeth Bowes-Lyon married the future George VI in 1923 at Westminster Abbey, she arranged for her bouquet to be laid on the grave of the Unknown Warrior, in remembrance of her brother Fergus who died in the First World War.

The Unknown Warrior

One of the most significant burials at Westminster Abbey is that of the Unknown Warrior. Following the death of nearly a million Britons in the First World War, the government decided to mark their combined sacrifice by burying the corpse of an unidentified soldier, who had fallen on the Western Front, at the west end of the Abbey's nave.

When the remains were brought to the Abbey for burial in 1920, more than a million people lined the streets as a sign of respect, underlining the pain that the war had brought to almost every family across the country.

The original inscription on the grave read simply: 'A British Warrior who fell in the Great War 1914 1918 for King and Country. Greater Love Hath No Man Than This'.

This gesture has been copied by every royal bride married at the Abbey since, and may form a part of William and Kate's ceremony.

Celebrating coronations

A *coronation* is when a new monarch is officially crowned, although the event is purely ceremonial. In fact, a new monarch's reign actually starts from when the previous one dies and not the coronation date – therefore Queen Elizabeth II has been the British monarch since 1952 even though her coronation was in 1953.

A gap always exists – sometimes of several months but often a year or more – between a monarch ascending the throne and the coronation taking place. The reason is because having a celebration too soon after the death of the previous monarch is considered bad taste. After all, the new monarch is very likely to be the son or daughter of the preceding monarch and may still be mourning.

A coronation is a celebration of a new monarch coming to the throne. The affair is very solemn but glitzy, with the monarch dressed in fine robes and jewels, overseen by the leading clergyman in the Church of England, the Archbishop of Canterbury.

All English, and later British, monarchs have had their coronations at Westminster Abbey, except one: the coronation of King Henry III in 1216 took place elsewhere because the French King Louis VIII had invaded London.

The Archbishop of Canterbury always crowns the new monarch who sits on the throne of Edward III, which dates back to the 14th century.

The throne is surprisingly plain and made of wood. At the time of coronation, the Stone of Scone (on which kings of Scotland were traditionally crowned) is placed under the throne. The stone symbolises the fact that the monarch crowned in Westminster is also the monarch of Scotland.

Marrying royals

No royal weddings were held at Westminster Abbey between 1382 and 1919 – with royals preferring to get hitched elsewhere – but in the 20th century the Abbey came back into vogue as the venue for the royal big day!

The late King George VI and Queen Elizabeth II tied the knot with their respective partners at the Abbey. Later, Princess Margaret (the Queen's now deceased sister), Anne, Princess Royal, and Prince Andrew, Duke of York, were married to their spouses there too.

Now William and Kate take their chance to have the happiest day of their lives at this magnificent building.

Prince William said that he and Kate chose Westminster Abbey because of its associations with his mother – who had her memorial service there – as well as what he called its 'staggering beauty' and 'feeling of a parish church'.

Westminster Abbey is considered such an important architectural and cultural site that it's one of the few buildings in Britain to hold UNESCO world heritage site status. And they don't give that honour to any old church or abbey!

Building the Abbey

Imagine building Wembley Stadium, the Olympic Stadium, the O2 arena and Buckingham Palace all at the same time! Pretty impossible job, yes? Well that's the equivalent of what King Henry III took on when he decided to rebuild Westminster Abbey in stone from 1245. A church had existed on the site for a few centuries; in fact, it was where the last Saxon king, Harold II, was crowned prior to his defeat by William the Conqueror at the Battle of Hastings.

King Henry's rebuilding of the Abbey was a massive undertaking and proved so costly – only the best would do for Henry – that it nearly bankrupted the country and special taxes had to be raised for the project.

The Abbey is built in a gothic Anglo-French style in a standard crucifix shape. It remained largely the same for five centuries until two towers were added on the western side of the building, designed by the great architect Nicholas Hawksmoor.

Fortunately the building survived the Second World War without substantial damage – some windows and masonry were damaged by German bombers in November 1940 – unlike the neighbouring Houses of Parliament, which suffered a direct hit.

The Abbey contains a shrine to Edward the Confessor who was King of England in the 11th century – before the Norman Invasion. He was considered a saint and the shrine became a place of pilgrimage in the Middle Ages.

Until the 19th century, Westminster Abbey was one of England's three great seats of learning – in other words, a university – along with Oxford and Cambridge.

Not many abbeys survive in Britain, mainly because King Henry VIII closed most of them down and stripped them of valuables. However, Westminster Abbey's roles as both a burial place of kings and a home to coronations and royal weddings undoubtedly saved it from Henry VIII's grasping hands.

Taking an Abbey Tour

If you want to visit Westminster Abbey, the easiest way is via the London Underground. The Abbey is a short walk from both Westminster and St James Park underground stations (turn to Chapter 7 for more on how to get around London on the big royal wedding day). Check out all the details at the Abbey's website, www.westminster-abbey.org.

If you fancy visiting the Abbey as a tourist, the entrance fee is £15 for adults and £6 for schoolchildren, although kids under 11 accompanied by an adult get in for free.

Looking at the Abbey's interior

Westminster Abbey wasn't just designed as a church – somewhere to perform daily services, weddings and burials – as an abbey it was a living institution and place of learning for the monks.

Looking its best for the big day

Westminster Abbey was one of the recipients of a £1 million grant by American bank Merrill Lynch. The restoration work funded by this donation will be complete in time for the royal wedding in April. Ten pieces will benefit from the grant, including coronation materials, rare medieval artifacts, manuscripts, books and drawings. Pieces include a wood panel portrait of Elizabeth I, silk embroidery panels from the coronation of Elizabeth II, and the coronation chair of Mary II.

For the wedding, William, Kate and their guests will enter through the Great West door into the giant nave of the church. If they look to their right they may see the Cloisters, which used to house the monks and abbots of the medieval Abbey. In the centre of the Cloisters is the Garth, an oasis of green. Beyond are other gardens and the smaller St Catherine's Cloister.

Farther into the Abbey are the stalls for the choir. On the right is Poet's Corner with its memorials to great writers and on the opposite side is the Great North door exit.

In the centre of this space is the shrine of Edward the Confessor and the sacrarium (sanctuary), which is where the high altar sits and ceremonies are performed. This area is very much the heart of the Abbey and where William and Kate will stand to be wed.

Behind this, at the back of the church and usually bathed in light shining through the Abbey's historic and beautiful stained glass, is Henry VII's Lady Chapel.

Figure 4-1 contains a layout of the Abbey.

Gazing at the treasures of the Abbey

The happy couple may not get time to appreciate them on their big day, but the Abbey contains a plethora of fine historic and artistic treasures. Here are some of the highlights:

- ✔ **The organ.** Originally built in 1727 and rebuilt four times since then, the Abbey's showpiece instrument is considered one of the finest in the country and will be played on William and Kate's special day.

✔ **The shrine.** By the sanctuary, the shrine contains the remains of several kings; nearby is the coronation throne of Edward III, which I describe in more detail in the earlier section 'Celebrating coronations'.

✔ **The Lady Chapel.** Containing the statues of no less than 95 saints, the chapel was built by Henry VII and is considered a great example of late medieval architecture. The Lady Chapel contains the tomb of Elizabeth I.

✔ **The Chapter House.** Containing sculptures and paintings depicting the Apocalypse and the Last Judgement, as well as the oldest door in Britain dating back to the 1050s, the Chapter House is where the monks used to pray and read from the Scriptures and other religious texts.

Bookshop **16**
Chapel of St. John the Baptist **6**
Chapel of St. John the Evangelist **5**
Chapter House **14**
Henry V's Chantry **8**
Poets' Corner **13**
Royal Air Force Chapel **11**
St. Andrew's Chapel **3**
St. Edward's Chapel
 (Coronation Chair) **7**

St. George's Chapel **1**
St. Michael's Chapel **4**
Tomb of Mary I &
 Elizabeth I **9**
Tomb of Henry VII **10**
Tomb of Mary,
 Queen of Scots **12**
Tomb of the Unknown Warrior/
 Memorial to Churchill **2**
Undercroft Museum **15**

Figure 4-1: Layout of the Abbey.

Chapter 5

Following the Rules of Etiquette

- -

In This Chapter

▶ The dress code – and the dress

▶ The order of precedence

▶ A guide to royal etiquette (should you meet the Queen)

- -

*E*tiquette is simply a code of behaviour, and it helps underpin some of the social norms of society. So for example, upon meeting someone for the first time, etiquette demands that you shake his or her hand as a sign of welcome.

Etiquette can get quite complex – and some would say plain daft – such as which knife to use at the dinner table or which way one should pass a bottle of port around the table. Much of the etiquette that we know today originated within the French royalty in the 17th and 18th centuries.

The rules of royal etiquette are a bit different from those that govern everyday etiquette and they exist to enforce a strict hierarchy and ensure royals can go about their business rather than being interrupted at any time.

This may all seem a bit much in our modern society and, indeed, the royal family is one of the few institutions where manners and protocol from the 19th century are alive and kicking.

But royal etiquette isn't about kowtowing; it's about respecting an institution which many would argue has served this country well. It's all about underlining the special nature of the relationship between the monarchy and the nation.

In this chapter, I take you on a quick tour of the tradition of etiquette that underpins the royal wedding.

On the wedding day, members of the royal household will be on hand to answer any questions guests may have about royal etiquette.

Dressing to Impress

Guests at the wedding are expected to behave with decorum and respect royal etiquette. In addition, a dress code will be enforced. It's not a night club. Muscular bouncers won't be positioned at the door ready to turn away anyone not correctly attired, but royal officials will be scrutinising guests, and those who don't comply with the dress code may not be allowed into the Abbey.

Trying to grab attention with a great big spectacular hat in church isn't going to go down well with the royals or other guests who have to duck for cover. Understatement is the key!

The dress code

The dress code will be as follows:

- ✔ Men can wear their military uniform or morning suits; lounge suits may also be allowable, but all with a tie, of course.

- ✔ Women need to stick to dresses – no miniskirts or sleeveless numbers – and hats.

Kate caused a bit of a wedding-attire stir in mid-January when she and Prince William attended the wedding of a long-time friend. Her stylish black dress that featured a sheer top had the tabloids abuzz about both the colour selection for a wedding (black) and the slightly risqué top (if you were to believe the tabloids). More importantly, the coverage confirmed that both she and her fashion choices are now firmly under the microscope.

The dress

Choice of dress is one of the key decisions of any wedding, and no discussion of wedding attire is complete with a bit about 'the dress'.

Guys are relatively easy to deal with. A smart suit and some shiny shoes normally suffice; although William may wed in his military uniform as previous royals often have – including his father. In the royal bride's case, though, the choice of gown is one for which the world is waiting with baited breath.

Bruce Oldfield has been selected to design the dress. The design and dress itself are to remain top secret until revealed when Kate emerges from her car onto the steps of Westminster Abbey itself on the big day – a traditional wedding-day surprise for Prince William and the world!

Almost as soon as the engagement was announced there was controversy over Kate's preferred designer, Daniella Helayel from Brazil. Journalists, British designers and even minor royal Viscountess Linley (Serena Armstrong-Jones, wife of Viscount Linley, son of the late Princess Margaret) argued that Kate ought to do the patriotic thing and buy British! Favourite Brit designers include world renowned names such as Alice Temperley, Dame Vivienne Westwood, and the ultimate winner, Oldfield.

Oldfield is a world-famous fashion designer and was Princess Diana's favourite. In addition to the Princess of Wales, he has dressed the likes of Sienna Miller, Barbara Streisand, Queen Rania of Jordan, and the staff of McDonald's. Yes, McDonald's. In 2008, Oldfield accepted a commission to redesign the uniforms for all McDonald's employees in Britain.

Princess Diana's wedding dress caused a sensation. It was designed by David and Elizabeth Emmanuel and had such a long train – 25 feet – that Diana's father couldn't fit in the glass coach which conveyed her to St Paul's.

Sorting Out the Order of Precedence

All weddings have an *order of precedence* – mum, dad and siblings in the front row of the church, near family behind them, more distant family members and their friends behind that and, of course, the best man standing at the front of the church looking nervous and thinking about the horrors of giving that speech.

Royal weddings – like all royal events – also have an order of precedence (in fact, I've heard that there's a strict order for opening Christmas presents). Such issues make worries about seating plans in most ordinary churches look like very small beer.

Normally at a wedding, the parents are top of the order of precedence, but at a royal wedding it's the Queen, who is William's grandmother.

Here's a run-down of the royal order of precedence:

- ✔ **The Queen:** Top of the tree is the Queen. She is the sovereign, and she'll sit in one of the seats reserved for the most important people in the Abbey.

- ✔ **Prince Philip:** Next is the Duke of Edinburgh, the Queen's husband, and grandfather to the prince.

- ✔ **The Queen's sons:** Prince Charles, Prince Andrew, Duke of York, and Prince Edward, Earl of Wessex, follow.

- ✔ **Prince Harry:** The Queen's other grandson comes next – William, of course, will be at the altar!

- ✔ **The male cousins of the Queen:** The Dukes of Gloucester and Kent and Prince Michael of Kent.

Notice a pattern here: no women so far apart from Her Majesty!

Next up are:

- ✔ **The eldest sons of the Queen's cousins:** The Earls of Ulster and St Andrews.

- ✔ **The younger sons of the Queen's cousins:** Lord Nicholas Windsor and Lord Frederick Windsor.

Then finally it's the turn of the female royals:

- ✔ **The Duchess of Cornwall and the Countess of Wessex:** The wives of Prince Charles and Prince Edward.

- ✔ **Anne the Princess Royal and Princess Alexandra:** The queen's daughter and cousin.

- ✔ **Princesses Eugenie and Beatrice:** The daughters of Prince Andrew.

- ✔ **The Duchesses of Gloucester and Kent and Princess Michael of Kent:** The wives of the Duke of Gloucester and Prince Michael of Kent.

- ✔ The Honourable Lady Ogilvy, Miss Zara Phillips, and the Countess of Ulster.

- ✔ The Lady Davina Lewis, The Lady Rose Gilman, and Countess of St Andrews.

- ✔ The Lady Nicholas Windsor, The Lady Helen Taylor, and The Lady Gabriella Windsor.

- ✔ And last but by no mean least, Mrs James Ogilvy and Miss Marina Ogilvy.

Royal precedence may seem arcane and strange to us – why can't they just sit where they want? And why should the grandmother have precedence over the father of the groom? However, the big idea behind it is that it gives greater importance to those who are closer to the throne or from an older generation.

For example, Prince Andrew is higher up the pecking order than Prince Harry, although Prince Harry is third in line to the throne and Andrew fourth. So it recognises seniority not just in terms of rank but also age.

And if you think that's quite a list already, it's just a small sample of all the royals who'll be attending; more distant relatives of the Queen from other countries will also be making an appearance.

Kate's family won't have to observe this strict order. On their side of the church, they'll enjoy a bit more seating freedom. And her proud mum and dad will be on the first pew.

Making a Big Entrance: The Queen and Royals

Plans call for the royal family to solemnly process into the Abbey to their seats after all the other guests have taken their seats but prior to the arrival of the bride. The royals will be in full regalia – so Her Majesty will be sporting her tiara.

Standing for the national anthem

'God save the Queen' – the proper version, not the one by the Sex Pistols – is usually included in the order of service to be sung during the ceremony. Guests will be expected to stand and sing the anthem. Usually, at a royal occasion, only the first two verses of the anthem are sung. Many people watching at home may also choose to stand and sing along, but don't worry if you've forgotten the words – the Queen can't see you!

Guests will stand as the royal party enters, each in order of precedence, until the Queen enters last. All the guests will remain standing until the royal entourage have taken their seats. With so many of them and those big robes, this part of the ceremony is likely to take quite a few minutes.

The entrance of the royal family should be quite a sight and one of the really interesting parts of the ceremony. The Royals don't just make an entrance on their own in silence. No, they'll be accompanied at a respectful distance by their *retinue*, including their heralds and staff as well as the clergy in attendance and the members of the choir. What's more, the sound of her trumpeters sounding a fanfare will accompany the entry of the Queen. It's all very grand – and it's meant to be.

Meeting the Queen

Some lucky souls may get the chance not only to see the Queen but to meet her on the big day. For that matter, enough royals will be milling about Westminster Abbey that the odds are even better for those in attendance of meeting some royal or another. There may even be a royal walkabout outside the Abbey, at which point onlookers can get into the action.

Without further ado, I include the official *For Dummies* do's and don'ts for meeting the Queen and other member of the royal family:

- ✔ Do curtsy if you're a woman.
- ✔ Do nod your head if you're a man.

- ✔ Don't worry about giving a curtsy or head nod if you're not British. You may prefer to get into the spirit of things and do it anyway.

- ✔ Don't talk to the royal unless you're spoken to.

- ✔ Don't grab their hand – or other part of the royal person – unless it is offered.

- ✔ Do shake the royal hand if it is offered but don't shake hands too firmly. The royals shake a lot of hands and don't want to end up with repetitive strain injury!

- ✔ Do call the Queen 'Your Majesty'. Upon second reference, 'Ma'am' is acceptable.

- ✔ Do call the other royals 'Your Highness'.

- ✔ Don't turn your back on a royal. It's considered disrespectful.

British people are officially called 'British subjects', which indicates that they're ruled by a monarch – hence all the curtsies and nods. The French, on the other hand, are called 'French citizens' because they're definitely not ruled by a monarch, having cut the heads off theirs a long time ago.

According to *Debrett's New Guide to Etiquette and Modern Manners* – essential holiday reading, I'm sure you'll agree – the full-on curtsy which involves descending all the way to the ground while shaking the hand of the monarch is now out of fashion. Instead, a brief bob with the weight on the front foot will do the job just fine. Now you know.

Tea with the Queen

If you're ever invited to tea with the Queen, the one golden rule is: as soon as Her Majesty stops chowing down, you need to stop, too. Not another bite. Not even if you're starving.

Chapter 6

Running Through the Day's Events

*T*he big day is 29 April. Every bride and groom experiences butterflies when they come face-to-face with the big 'I do'. But just imagine dealing with the small matter of a billion plus people watching it all on television.

Like any wedding day nothing can be allowed to go wrong. An event as big as a royal wedding has to run like clockwork. Think of the day like a swan swimming in a lake. All is calm and dignified up top, but beneath the surface there's bound to be a mad scramble of feet to remain buoyant.

In this chapter, I take you behind the scenes with the royal wedding planners and set out what will happen on the big day from the moment Westminster Abbey is opened to the point at which the last glass of champagne has been enjoyed at the evening's dinner.

Getting Things in Order at the Abbey

Wedding guests – all 1,800 of them – are expected to have taken their seats at Westminster Abbey at least an hour before the ceremony begins at 11:00.

After the non-dignitary portion of the guest list is seated, the dignitaries will enter the Abbey. These individuals include members of other royal families, leading British politicians and ambassadors and representatives from other countries.

After the dignitaries find their seats, the royals will file into the Abbey, in a strict order of precedence (which I outline in Chapter 5). Last of the royals to enter will be the Queen. Her Majesty will take her seat at the left hand end of the front row to the right of the altar.

When the Queen is seated, a message will be sent to Kate and her father, Michael Middleton, at which point they'll depart for Westminster Abbey.

Leaving for the Abbey

Kate Middleton is scheduled to leave Buckingham Palace or Clarence House (the home of Prince Charles) for Westminster Abbey at 10:30. Her father will accompany her on the trip.

Breaking with tradition, Kate will travel with her father to the Abbey in a limo – no, not one of those stretch party limos you see in city centres on a Saturday night, but something a bit more tasteful and understated. The choice of a limo is unusual because previous royal brides travelled to their weddings in a royal carriage. Princess Diana, for example, went in a carriage made with gold and glass – very Cinderella! But Kate wants something a little more low key, and a limo does have the advantage of keeping the wind out of her hair!

The trip from the Palace to the Abbey is only a very short distance (barely a mile), but the car will drive slowly and may take some time to cover the distance swinging around the edge of St James's Park, through Horse Guard's Parade and down Whitehall to Parliament Square. This route will give onlookers a good chance for their first glimpse of Kate on her big day. (See Chapter 7 for more on the best places along the route to see the events.)

The moment that Kate arrives at Westminster Abbey and steps out of the limo will be one of the most photo-graphed events of the year, second only to the point at which the couple emerge from the Abbey together. Why? Because Kate's emergence from the car will be the first time the world gets to see her wedding dress in all its finery.

Taking in the Main Event: The Ceremony

With all of the excitement and hype, it's easy to forget what the whole day is really about – the wedding cer-emony itself; when two individuals pronounce their love for one another and their desire to be husband and wife.

The essentials of the ceremony are no different to any ordinary wedding service. The service will be Anglican and contain prayers, readings and hymns.

First, though, the bride must make her entrance. Kate's walk down the aisle of Westminster Abbey is likely to take around four minutes, bearing in mind the length of the Abbey and the fact that she'll be wearing a huge wedding dress. Music will accompany Kate on her walk down the aisle. If I were a betting man, I wouldn't put my money on 'Here Comes the Bride' (from Wagner's opera *Lohengrin*, music fans). Instead, expect it to be classical music played on the Abbey's historic organ (see Chapter 4 for more on this instrument).

The wedding service itself will be conducted by not one but three reverends:

- **The Dean of Westminster:** The Very Reverend John Hall, the 38th Dean of Westminster Abbey, will conduct the service.

- **The Archbishop of Canterbury:** Dr Rowan Williams, the 104th Archbishop of Canterbury, will then marry the couple.

- **The Bishop of London:** Finally, the Right Reverend John Chartres will address the congregation.

Not a bad line up!

The service with the vows and the exchange of rings is meant to start at 11:00 and is expected to last an hour or just over.

William – more than likely in his RAF uniform – will be waiting at the altar with best man Prince Harry.

Something to watch for: ever since the First World War, royal brides have followed the tradition of laying their wedding bouquet on the Tomb of the Unknown Warrior in Westminster Abbey after the service. This is a touching mark of respect to all those who have lost their lives fighting for this country. (See Chapter 4 for more about the tomb and the ins and outs of historic Westminster Abbey.)

Proceeding Back to the Palace

With their vows stated, rings exchanged and the sounds of the final hymn filling their ears, Kate and William will walk out of the Abbey as man and wife. This is the ultimate Kodak moment for the crowds that will be gathered outside the Abbey.

The couple will then step into a royal carriage – no limo on the way back – and return to Buckingham Palace along the same route that Kate travelled barely more than an hour or so before. They won't be alone, though. The Queen's Household Cavalry will escort the couple on horseback.

Cranking Up the Party Spirit

Upon their return to Buckingham Palace, Kate and William will do what ordinary couples do on their wedding day – prepare for the reception with their wedding guests.

Well, almost. There's the small matter of posing for official photographs for distribution to the world's media as the guests arrive.

A large number of guests will attend the reception at Buckingham Palace, and the kitchens will be a hive of activity. The couple have taken the highly unusual step – in royal circles, that is – of asking for a buffet to be organised.

The Queen is known to not enjoy a buffet – in fact, a story goes that she once attended a wedding buffet and asked that her and Prince Philip have a sit down meal brought to them. But what wedding wouldn't be complete without at least one disagreement in the family!

There's no official confirmation yet, but it would be a major surprise if the happy couple and other members of the royal family didn't make an appearance on the balcony at Buckingham Palace at some point during the reception. Both Prince Charles and Prince Andrew made such appearances with their new brides – Lady Diana and Sarah Ferguson – on their respective wedding days. If Kate and William make an appearance, it will be a major moment in the day because the Mall outside Buckingham Palace will be packed with well wishers.

Prince William is rumoured to have requested an RAF flypast at some point during the day. Whether it would occur during the reception is still up in the air.

The wedding – Sylvanian style

It seems that Wills and Kate aren't the only ones tying the knot in April. Also on the cards is the wedding of William and his bride Catherine, two brown-eared rabbits and the centerpiece of the Sylvanian Families Wedding Set. (If you're reading this on the other side of the Atlantic, you may know the Sylvanian Families as the Calico Critters, those popular miniature animals beloved by children.) The Reverend Kelvin Waters, a beaver, will preside.

Wrapping Up the Day: The Private Function

The reception will take several hours. With official photographs and the likelihood of a balcony appearance, Kate and William may not have as much time to spend with their guests as they'd like, which is often the way at weddings.

Unlike most weddings though, after the reception Prince Charles will host another party for family members and close friends. Dancing will be on the bill at this event, but don't expect a Dancing Queen to hit the floor and bust some moves. She and Prince Philip are unlikely to attend the evening shindig as it will be a more raucous affair than the earlier reception.

The wedding reception is being paid for by the Queen with the Middletons chipping in – after all, they are millionaires. However, the costs of security and crowd control on the day – estimated to be at least £10 million – will be paid for by the taxpayer – that's you and me! So much for the idea that we're getting a 'free' holiday from work on the day!

Part III

Taking Part in the Festivities

'And how shall I book your flight to London—First Class, Coach, or Medieval?'

In this part . . .

*H*ere, I provide you with a host of suggestions and tips for organising a fun royal wedding day. Whether you're travelling to London for the big day or partying closer to home, you've come to the right part. I include a guide to getting around London, tips on throwing a street party to remember and a few fantastic recipes that are sure to impress. Finally, I top it off with a right royal quiz for you to have some fun with after the vows.

Chapter 7

The Best Places to View the Events

*I*f you're planning to watch the royal wedding in person, the key is to get your pitch on the route *early* and know where you're most likely to get the best vantage point. Arrive late or get your location wrong, and you could end up spending a few frustrating hours looking at the back of a fellow reveller's head rather than Wills and Kate.

However early you plan to arrive at your chosen perch, though, you can bet your bottom dollar that someone will be there before you. It's not unusual to find some hardy souls camped out days before a big royal event in order to secure prime position.

In this chapter, I go through some of the prime locations to get as good a view as possible of the royal wedding, taking in the undoubtedly unique atmosphere and seeing a few of London's most famous sights into the bargain.

If you want to see the events in person and you haven't been one of the lucky few to receive an invite, this chapter is a must read. And be sure to check out www.dummmies.com, which features video footage of me touring some of these locations.

Kate will travel by car to the ceremony, but a carriage
will perform the honour on the way back to the palace. So
the return trip should provide the crowds the best views
of the happy couple.

Buckingham Palace

This is *the* ideal location for getting two bites of the royal
wedding cherry. Not only does the soon-to-be-married
Kate set off from the Queen's official London residence
(or from Clarence House next door), but the happily
married couple are scheduled to return later for the
reception to end all receptions.

The area around the Palace is ideal to cope with the
inevitable crowds, with wide, sweeping boulevards
and a stunning vista across the iconic fountain outside
Buckingham Palace to St James's Park and the Mall
beyond.

Be aware, though, that apart from Westminster Abbey
itself, this will be the prime spot for royal wedding
watchers so be prepared for a crush.

Clarence House

Clarence House, the residence of the Prince of Wales,
is smaller and more intimate than Buckingham Palace.
Set back from the Mall – but without the grand scale or
parade ground of Buckingham Palace – this could be the
spot to catch the first glimpse (through a car window) of
the dress that Kate will be wearing.

Position yourself as close as possible to the gate house on the Mall entrance. If the limo emerges from Clarence House, spectators located near the gate house will only be yards away and catch the first public glimpse of Kate on her wedding day.

The Mall

Crowds will be allowed to stand on both sides of the Mall – the main thoroughfare leading from Buckingham Palace and Clarence House to Westminster and the Abbey. The cars carrying Kate and the royals will in all likelihood take this route to and from the service.

On a big royal occasion such as a wedding, coronation or jubilee, the Mall is a great place to be because its width and openness provide an ideal viewing opportunity. In addition to the views of the cars and carriages the Mall will afford, if the royal family choose to come onto the balcony at Buckingham Palace on the big day, they'll be clearly visible from the Mall.

Often on wedding days, after the royal family is back in Buckingham Palace and attending the reception, police remove the crash barriers keeping the crowds on either side of the Mall, allowing the crowds to fill the space. So if you want a second look at the happy couple, head over to the Mall and join in the throng of flag-waving admirers.

St James's Park

Nestled between the beating hearts of Westminster and Buckingham Palace, the attractions of St James's Park as a vantage point for the big royal wedding are obvious.

But the park is big – 58 acres to be precise. If you're at the centre of the park on the banks of the lake you won't see much apart from the crowd in front of you.

In the park, locate yourself either facing the Mall or Horse Guard's Parade. Here, you'll have a chance of spotting Kate and the royals twice as they move from the Palace and Clarence House to Westminster Abbey.

If it proves to be a hot and sunny day (and there's no guarantee; see the nearby sidebar 'Rain or shine?'), St James's Park could prove an ideal spot because the trees that grace its grounds can provide shade from the sun.

Rain or shine?

You've probably heard the phrase 'April showers', but what are the chances of the thousands of well-wishers being shortchanged by Britain's famously unpredictable climate?

London in April typically gets about 190 hours of sunshine – which is 60 hours more than March – and the average temperature on 29 April over the last 20 years, according to the Met Office, is a fairly pleasant 17 degrees Celsius (that's 63 degrees Fahrenheit). It's hardly shirt-sleeve weather, but neither is it cold enough to dust off the winter coat.

Roughly speaking, the MET Office say that a 1 in 3 chance exists for London to see some rain on the wedding day. However, the chances of a complete wash out with heavy rain all day are a lot less worrisome 1 in 30. So, all in all, it looks like the weather should be set fair.

But no one can be *absolutely* sure what the weather will be like on the big day – this is Britain after all – so if you're going, pack an umbrella, a warm drink in a flask and dress in layers, including a good wind-resistant waterproof.

Horse Guards Parade

Horse Guards Parade has a number of positive points that should make it a great vantage point for royal watching:

- ✔ Horse Guards Parade is located equidistant between the Palace and the Abbey.

- ✔ The big open area of the Parade – it's used to coping with thousands of tourists a day – could be a less crowded spot than either the Mall or outside Buckingham Palace.

- ✔ Spectators may be allowed to make use of the stands which occupy the eastern part of the parade ground.

  Stands are often erected here because Horse Guards Parade is the site of the annual Trooping the Colour ceremony, which commemorates the birthday of the reigning monarch.

Horse Guards Parade is the only vantage point for the royal wedding that is also a venue for the 2012 London Olympics. The Parade will host the beach volleyball competition, although they may not let you camp out for that one.

Whitehall

The streets of Whitehall, at the centre of British government, should provide another vantage point for people not wanting to brave the crowds of Westminster Abbey or Buckingham Palace. Crowds here will be able to see the royal cars as they proceed through Horse Guards Parade and onto Parliament Square.

Like Clarence House, Whitehall will be an intimate location with watchers perhaps only a few yards away from Kate and the royals as they slowly proceed past. Get those cameras ready!

Parliament Square

This green space is outside the northwest square of the Houses of Parliament (also known as the Palace of Westminster) – one of the world's iconic buildings. It will provide views of Kate and the royals arriving as they have to proceed all the way around the square to arrive at Westminster Abbey.

Crowds here will also be able to see the newlyweds as they emerge from the Abbey in the distance.

Trees in the west of Parliament Square can provide shade if the sun shines!

Westminster Abbey

This is the place to be if you want to be at the heart of the action.

The crowds will be massive but the rewards will be great. Westminster Abbey may be your best opportunity to get a glimpse of all the guests arriving, along with William and Kate as they emerge from the Abbey as newlyweds. Potentially it's the photo opportunity of a lifetime.

Where to locate yourself on the day? Crowds will be kept reasonably clear of the two entrances to the Abbey (no shaking the couple's hands or throwing confetti as they emerge, I'm afraid) but will be allowed to stand behind crash barriers at a distance.

Get there *early*!

Hyde Park

It's not on the royal wedding route, but Hyde Park will no doubt be a great place to be on the big day. London's biggest park, at over 240 acres, is often a place of national celebration.

There are bound to be lots of people looking to enjoy the day in the park, and red, white and blue will be everywhere. There are plans – although not yet confirmed at the time I'm writing this – to show the wedding on a big screen in the park and the possibility of a music concert to follow. (Check out Chapter 11 for a host of websites that will keep you up to date on all the latest royal wedding news and events.)

Even if the weather isn't perfect, Hyde Park is a great place to listen to music and will be no doubt a centre of royal wedding celebrations on 29 April.

In Your Front Room

Let's face it: only a tiny fraction of those who want to take part in the big day will be able to stand with the crowds in London.

But never fear – the royal wedding will be broadcast on BBC1, ITV and Sky News – and on television stations throughout the world. And if you miss any of the live event – and I can't think why you'd want to go and do that – highlight programmes will be shown in the evening.

Chapter 8

Throffng a Proper Street Party

● ●

In This Chapter

▶ Enjoying a street party

▶ Remembering some great street parties

▶ Organising your own street party

▶ Clearing up afterwards

● ●

*A*lthough the British have a reputation for being reserved, they're not all stiff upper lips and aching formality. Not a bit of it. Occasionally they like to let their hair down – just don't let the rest of the world know!

One noticeable such occasion is the traditional British street party, where tables are hauled into the street, bunting hung from lampposts, and food, soft drinks and the odd glass of something stronger is served. And a royal wedding is a great reason to hold a street party.

In this chapter I examine the phenomenon of the Great British Street Party – past and present – and give you some handy pointers to organising your own for William and Kate's big day (you may surprised at just how much is involved). Break out the bunting, it's party time!

Looking at Why People Love Street Parties

The UK has a long tradition of holding street parties to mark significant events and major royal occasions. Although most countries love a festival or a carnival, Britons are particularly fond of the street party. Here are some possible reasons why:

- ✔ Britain is densely populated – lots of people live in terraced housing next to one another, which is the ideal environment for a street party.

- ✔ A collective memory of street parties of the past makes it seem the natural thing to do.

- ✔ A lot of popular TV programmes and soap operas depict the holding of street parties, such as *Eastenders* and *Coronation Street*, reinforcing the idea that they're traditional.

Whatever the reason for Britain's love of the street party, one thing's for sure: the marriage of Prince William to Catherine Middleton is going to prompt a whole host of them up and down the country – perhaps even in your street.

Taking in Great Street Parties of the Past

For many Brits a street party isn't just here today, gone tomorrow; it's the stuff of memories for years to come. One of my earliest memories is going to a street party with my mum and celebrating the Silver Jubilee (in 1977).

The day was hot and glorious: people were dancing, flags were flying everywhere and I'm pretty sure I drank far too much orange squash.

Royal occasions aren't the only ones to merit a street party; many impromptu local parties are organised to celebrate particular events or alongside annual village fetes. Any excuse for a party!

Street parties can be a real touchstone in individual and collective memory; here are some of the Great British shindigs of the past.

Celebrating victory: VE Day, 1945

You have to be at least 70 years old to remember this street party occasion, but it was supposedly a cracker.

VE Day – 8 May 1945 – stands for Victory in Europe day; Britain had emerged from six years of bloody war, battered, bruised but not beaten. The country, which had come within a hair's-breadth of invasion, breathed a massive sigh of relief.

Although food shortages and rationing were still in place, the Brits saw the end of the war as an ideal reason to party – and who can blame them!

Crowning a monarch: The Queen's coronation, 1953

The young Queen Elizabeth II had been on the throne for a year at the time of her coronation at Westminster Abbey (read Chapter 4 for more on this great building, the venue for William and Kate's wedding).

Not only was the coronation unusual in that Elizabeth was the first queen to be crowned in well over a century, but also it was unique in being the first coronation to be broadcast on television.

Unlike today, TVs were fairly scarce – in fact a television cost the equivalent of £5,000 in today's money – but most streets had at least one home with a set. So families from up and down the street grouped around that TV to watch the magical spectacle and then went out afterwards for a good old-fashioned street party.

Dancing in the streets 1: The Queen's Silver Jubilee, 1977

The 25th anniversary of Queen Elizabeth II ascending the throne was a major national celebration. A public holiday was declared and people revived memories of VE Day and the coronation by organising street parties.

Like now, Britain in 1977 was emerging from a period of severe economic turbulence and people seemed determined to have a good time.

The Wimbledon tennis championships even managed to produce a British winner – Virginia Wade – to cap the festivities.

Getting hitched: Prince Charles and Lady Diana's wedding, 1981

The marriage of William's father and mother was a great excuse for a national celebration with street parties taking centre stage.

1981 was a difficult year for the UK with widespread riots and 3,000,000 people unemployed. Britons wanted a reason to forget their woes and the marriage of Prince Charles to the beautiful Lady Diana Spencer provided the perfect excuse.

The fairytale romance ended tragically (check out Chapter 3 for more details), but such an outcome was far from the minds of the millions of people enjoying their street parties on that hot summer day in 1981.

Dancing in the streets II: The Queen's Golden Jubilee, 2002

For thousands of Britons, the Golden Jubilee was another royal red-letter day and another excuse for a street party. The Queen has always been a hugely popular figure and so her achievement of 50 years on the throne touched many around the country.

The number of street parties may not have been as great as for the Silver Jubilee or Charles and Diana's wedding, but nevertheless a fair old amount of feasting and fun took place.

Yet another royal reason for a street party arises in 2012, when the Queen celebrates her Diamond Jubilee (or 60 years on the throne). So hold onto this guide to street parties!

Checking Off the Street Party Essentials

Unfortunately, organising a street party isn't as simple as moving a few tables into the street, making sandwiches and mixing the punch – although all that needs to be done. In these times of health and safety and parking restrictions, in large parts of the UK official permission has to be sorted and insurance purchased.

But don't fear, many of the necessary tasks can be done through your local council or by speaking to local businesses – and this section helps by providing loads of tips and ideas on arranging a street party, such as:

- ✔ Organising your neighbours and distributing the workload.
- ✔ Securing sponsorship from local businesses.
- ✔ Finding the right music to make the party swing.
- ✔ Taking care of food and drink.
- ✔ Getting hold of the right insurance.
- ✔ Checking out whether you need a licence.

Planning a street party is a major undertaking that can take a while to organise properly, and so you'd better get started now!

Getting the neighbours involved

Often the hardest part of organising a street party is co-opting friends and neighbours into helping out. You know the story: everyone thinks that having a party would be lovely, but only a handful of people want to help.

However, don't despair. A bit of door knocking or attendance at a local Neighbourhood Watch meeting should enable you to drum up sufficient bodies to man the stores, serve the drinks, put up tables and tidy away after.

On the day, make sure that all volunteers know their jobs so that you don't have ten people catering and no one doing the tidying up. If the party is well planned and people know what they're doing, the day is much more likely to be successful. Here are a couple of ideas to help with your planning:

  ✔ Form a Facebook page on the Internet ahead of your big party and invite friends and neighbours to join. The page helps keep everyone up to date with the planning.

  ✔ Organise a committee to oversee the preparations for the party, and ask volunteers to take on certain roles such as publicity, procurement or catering. Look to harness the special abilities of each person; for example, if you have an accountant in your street, ask him or her to be treasurer (check out the later section 'Getting the finances right').

Making ends meet

Unless you're financially loaded and want to share your good fortune with your neighbours by paying for a street party, most likely you want to raise a little revenue to cover the costs.

Here are some ideas for spreading the cost burden:

- ✔ Ask neighbours for an upfront contribution, but if you do, remember to keep receipts of all your expenditure so you can produce them if asked.

- ✔ Charge a participation fee on the day; say, a couple of pounds or a flat fee for a whole household. These contributions soon add up; you may even turn a profit to donate to a good cause that's been agreed in advance.

- ✔ Sell alcohol on the day, but remember that you may require a temporary licence – flip to the later section 'Doing it the right way: Licensing' for more info.

- ✔ Try to get a sponsor, such as a prominent local business, to help supply alcohol, food or other necessities to create a party to remember.

Estate agency chains are a good source of sponsorship for local events – where I live in West London, they often support local school sports days. They get a name-check on any literature or on the bunting and in return they hand over some readies; job done!

Laying down some music for the day

A party isn't a party without music. On the day itself mobile discos are going to be in high demand, which may mean they charge more and are booked up early. An alternative is to see whether a neighbour is handy at DJing – hiring the equipment and having that person handle the decks may well be cheaper.

Another option is to see whether a friend or neighbour is a musician or part of a band. Seeing a familiar face strumming a guitar or beating a drum can be really good fun. A good street party is as much about harnessing local character and talent as about downing the punch and scoffing the sandwiches (although don't forget that too!).

Ideally, your party is going to attract and entertain all age groups, and so make sure that the choice of music is as broad as possible. At the risk of offending any 80-year-old rave fans, a 'hard house' set is unlikely to appeal to octogenarians and four hours of Glenn Miller won't get the kids dancing. (Music choice is something more easily controlled with a DJ rather than a live band.)

If you have no DJ or live band, borrow a neighbour's sound system, connect an MP3 player and pre-programme a party playlist of tunes. Include some standard floor fillers that no party can be without, such as Abba and The Beatles. Check out official Internet download sites to see what's on their party album selection.

Just be careful about keeping the music system dry and safe from any potential criminal element – that may come from outside your street, of course!

Catering to the masses

If you want an ultra-posh party, you can hire a catering company to supply the food on the day – this firm may well also offer the option of waiter service and no doubt do all the clearing up.

This option can prove very costly, however, and many street residents may question whether the expense is a waste of money.

Get three different catering company quotes for comparison. Don't just accept the cheapest though; have a taste of the food on offer and see which you prefer.

An alternative is to get a local deli to prepare some food – lasagna, moussaka and chilli are all good party fare and you can order large quantities. Delis can also supply sandwiches and rolls, for those who prefer more traditional British food. You can pick up the plates of food in the morning and return them empty in the evening. Again, though, the deli option is more expensive than doing it yourself.

If you get a local deli involved, try and strike a sponsorship deal with them so that everyone knows where the delicious food is from; you may get a little money knocked off.

Of course, the cheapest food option is getting different volunteers to muck in, each taking responsibility for different dishes. This approach can be serious fun with households comparing their cakes and sandwiches. And you may even find that you have a secret Jamie Oliver or Nigella Lawson hidden in your street!

If you're all sharing the responsibilities for the catering, make sure that everyone involved keeps receipts. This system ensures that people can get a refund if you're holding a central kitty (turn to 'Getting the finances right', later in this chapter for more on finances).

Insuring yourself against the unexpected

Although insurance seems like the least party-like subject in the world, you do have to think about it as regards your street party. Here's why:

✔ Someone may injure themselves on the day, which is more likely if you're arranging extra events such as tug of war (flip to the later section 'Piling on the fun: Extra events'.)

✔ Somebody may commit theft or damage – someone from outside the street, of course!

✔ The event may be rained off completely and the organisers left with a big bill, but no money from attendees or drink sales.

Although the weather in late April can be good over much of the UK, the risk of showers is ever present. Therefore, make sure that you have bad-weather contingency plans in place.

Perhaps retain the option of hosting the party indoors at a local hall or community centre. At the very least, suggest to attendees that they dress up warm for the occasion.

Fingers crossed, most things will go to plan but you have to be prepared for the unexpected. A single-day insurance policy to cover any of the eventualities listed above is easy to buy; try www.biba.org.uk for a list of local insurance brokers, or contact specialist events insurers (such as www.hiscox.co.uk/events or www.events-insurance.co.uk).

Shop around for the best insurance deal; get at least three quotes and compare the level of cover each company offers. You may be best going for the more expensive option if, for example, you're then covered for physical events such as races or a game of rounders – better to be safe than sorry.

Although unlikely, in theory if someone is injured at your street party you can be sued. Don't take the risk: check out your insurance options.

Doing it the right way: Licensing

Usually, street parties don't require an event licence from the local council, which is good news because the bureaucracy can send your head into a spin! However, if you plan to charge an admission fee or sell alcohol, you may need to apply for Temporary Event Notice at least two weeks before the party.

Local rules differ, and so do give your council a call to check.

Instead of selling alcohol at the event, why not place beer and wine on a table with a sign saying, 'Suggested donation: £1 for a beer, £2 for a glass of wine'. In this way you aren't, strictly speaking, selling alcohol.

As a courtesy, let your local police station know that you're planning to hold a street party. They may even want to send a community police officer down to help with the event – a burly copper may be quite handy!

Protecting the party: Road closures

Traffic would be a major problem for your street party. You don't want to start off the festivities only for the post van or bin lorry to turn into your road, scattering the first row of tables.

In fact, organising an official road closure is fairly easy, particularly because your local authority is sure to be geared-up for street parties on William and Kate's big day!

As long as you invite every house in the street – so don't leave anyone out – the council deems that you've consulted all your neighbours about the road closure.

You need to apply to the council's highway department for permission to close the road, and you need to do so at least four weeks before the big day.

The council is likely to consult the local police, fire and ambulance services to check whether they have any objections to the closure. If, for example, you have a residential care home on your street, the ambulance service may object on the grounds that they need 24-hour access. In most cases, however, gaining permission is plain sailing.

Some councils charge a small permission fee – mine charges £25, which hardly seems worthwhile – but they are the council, after all!

On the event day, you need signage to indicate that the road is closed. The council may have some spare signs to lend you or they may charge you to buy one – expect to pay around £50. You can also make supplementary signs yourself to display so that motorists well and truly get the message.

As a courtesy, post a note to everyone in the street letting them know the details of the closure. This way, anyone who wants to leave the street – say, to visit family or even to attend the royal wedding itself – is aware of when they can move their vehicle.

If you can't close the road fully – perhaps because someone in the road needs 24-hour emergency vehicle access – investigate holding the party on the pavement or a patch of green communal space.

Piling on the fun: Extra events

You may have a mental image of your street party: lots of happy neighbours sat at long tables gorging on goodies and chatting. But this may not be enough to keep everyone amused. Kids, for example, don't garner the same enjoyment from food and conversation as adults and can get easily bored.

You can organise some events to run before and after the eating and drinking, to hold people's interest for longer and make a full day of the festivities.

You can charge an entry fee for some of these extra events as a way to raise cash for charity or help the costs of the party.

Here are some suggestions for extra events on the royal wedding day:

- ✔ **Egg and spoon race:** Contestants race each other carrying a spoon with an egg balanced precariously on it.

- ✔ **Bring and buy sale:** This stall can help raise extra cash; basically people bring stuff they don't want anymore and sell it.

- ✔ **Tug of war:** This old favourite has two teams pulling against each other on a rope until a point marked on the rope reaches a specific point and a winning team is declared. Be warned though, things can get quite competitive!

- ✔ **Sack race:** Yes, another race, but this time contestants have to hop along the course in a sack; a great way to look very silly indeed!

✔ **Rounders:** If you have some green space in your street, organise a game of rounders; people of all ages can take part because the rules are very easy to pick up.

✔ **Best cake competition:** This event is cheating a little because everyone gets to tuck into the contestants' entries after the competition, helping to take care of some of the catering. Yet, who's complaining?

✔ **Tombola:** This event is basically a raffle; you buy a ticket that entitles you to a prize. Everyone's a winner! (Which is, incidentally, also a must-have party song for your music playlist!)

✔ **Royal quiz:** I just so happen to provide 100 questions and answers and guidance on organising a quiz in Chapter 10 . . . how convenient!

Try to assign the job of organising each extra event to an individual – so, for example, David from Number 17 handles the tombola while Mavis from Number 38 organises the sack race. Giving responsibility to an individual usually ensures that each event goes swimmingly.

In case of injury, try to ensure that a trained first-aider (holding an up-to-date first aid certificate) is on standby. If you're having a large party, or including more physically-risky events such as a tug of war, the St John Ambulance may want to attend. Check out www.sja. org.uk for more details.

Watching the main event

As you get caught up in organising your street party, don't forget what it's all about – the royal wedding! You need to figure out how everybody's going to watch the action from Westminster Abbey. Here are a few ideas:

✔ The simplest option is to schedule the party so that it precedes or follows the royal wedding, thus ensuring that everyone can enjoy the spectacle from the comfort of their own homes.

✔ You can erect a large television screen for everyone to watch, but be aware of the potential for damage; also, you may have to hire a big-screen TV if you want everyone to see, which can be very expensive.

✔ You can ask your neighbours to bring out a TV set each, so that people have lots of screens to watch while enjoying the party; however, this option means lots of wires and the potential for accidents.

Ask your neighbours and fellow party organisers how they prefer to watch the main event: do they want to view it at home or together on the street?

Getting the finances right

Even if you've secured sponsorship or thought of some clever schemes to raise cash (as I describe in the earlier section 'Making ends meet'), you still need someone to oversee the finances of the whole project – in other words, to keep the books. This is where a treasurer comes in. Here's a list of some of the vital work that person can do to make sure that the finances of the party are as sound as a pound:

✔ Keep a record of all outgoings and incomings.

✔ Ensure that all organisers supply all receipts.

✔ Collect any profits and pay this amount to the organisers or the chosen good cause, as agreed in advance.

> ✔ Keep all the party's receipts and accounts for at
> least six years in case the tax authorities want to
> investigate the finances of the party.

HM Revenue and Customs (HMRC) is very unlikely to
investigate the finances of a royal wedding party, but
nevertheless officers have the right to do so for six years
after the event.

Picking Up the Pieces: The Clear-up

Every good party ends in the clear-up (just recall the
scenes of devastation at the end of the Woodstock
festival in 1969!). Of course, clearing up is no fun but you
can make it less of a chore with some simple dos and
don'ts for the end of the party:

✔ Do identify which organisers are going to help with
the clear-up.

✔ Don't saddle those who've worked hard in the
run-up to the party with the job of clearing up.

✔ Do organise the people clearing up into teams so
that some are responsible for rubbish disposal and
recycling, others for sweeping the street and others
for clearing the tables.

✔ Don't use lots of crockery or glass – they're a nightmare
to clean – use paper plates and cups that can be
recycled.

✔ Do put your rubbish in the correct colour bins and
look to recycle as much as possible: a good party
needn't cost the earth!

Don't employ a professional cleaning company unless you're loaded; they charge a fortune. The clear-up may look daunting, but a few enthusiastic volunteers can get things done in double-quick time.

Chapter 9

Party Fare Fit for a King

*N*o two parties are going to be alike come wedding day – except for the requisite large-screen telly – so I include two very different types of food here for your consideration. First, I focus on party food – you can think of it as an international twist on pub grub – for a casual affair. But if your plans tend more towards formal dress and good china, check out the second part of this chapter.

Note: The recipes in this chapter often serve two to four people. Simply scale them as necessary to feed your crowd.

Digging into Delicious Dips and Snacks

The recipes in this section are perfect if you're planning a laid back event or you're looking for dishes with a bit of international flair. I've made a point to include plenty of easy-to-assemble party foods so you can spend more time enjoying watching the ceremony and less time in the kitchen.

Global dips sure to satisfy

Dips are super-easy to whip up. If you're looking for something to nibble on throughout the day – crisps, breadsticks or sliced vegetables – the dips in this section are perfect for friends and family.

Blue Cheese and Chive Dip

Cheesier than the hairstyle you had when Charles and Diana tied the knot, this dip is a must for all cheese (and chive) fans. Very quick to make and great with a few crisps or Ryvitas.

Preparation time: 5 minutes • **Cooking time:** Nil • **Serves:** 2

Ingredients	*Directions*
4 spoonfuls of mayonnaise	Add all the ingredients into a large bowl and mix together. Serve.
100 grams (about a fistful) of grated blue cheese (Roquefort, Stilton or St Agur)	
Big pinch of chopped chives (fresh if possible, dried don't really work)	
Grind of pepper	
Squeeze of lemon juice	
1 spoonful of double cream (optional)	

Per serving: Calories 453 (From Fat 399); Fat 44.3g (Saturated 17.4g); Cholesterol Trace; Sodium 531mg; Carbohydrate 1.0g, Dietary Fibre 0.1g; Protein 12.5g.

Guacamole

Guacamole is a great Mexican dip made from avocados.

Preparation time: 10 to 15 minutes • **Cooking time:** Nil • **Serves:** 4

Ingredients	*Directions*
2 tomatoes	*1* Cut the tomatoes in half and scoop out the seeds with a spoon. Finely chop the tomatoes.
1 chilli (red or green, doesn't matter) or some Tabasco sauce	*2* Chop the top off the chilli, slice in half lengthways and remove the seeds. Now finely chop and add to the tomatoes.
3 large avocados	
1 clove of garlic, peeled and crushed	*3* Remove the avocado stone and, using a spoon, scoop out the flesh into a clean bowl and add the lemon juice. Mash the mixture to your preferred consistency – chunky or smooth.
¼ medium onion, finely chopped	
2 to 3 tablespoons of lemon juice	*4* Add the chilli (or Tabasco), tomato and onion and mix well.
Salt and pepper	*5* Season with salt and pepper to taste. You may need to add a bit more lemon juice. If not using it immediately, cover tightly with cling film and place in the fridge.

Per serving: Calories 243 (From Fat 200); Fat 22.2g (Saturated 4.7g); Cholesterol Trace; Sodium 38mg; Carbohydrate 7.6g, Dietary Fibre 5.0g; Protein 3.1g.

Hummus

Hummus, made from puréed chickpeas, is a dish from the Middle East. It's a really easy dip to make, although for best results, use a blender.

Preparation time: 10 minutes • **Cooking time:** Nil • **Serves:** 2

Ingredients	*Directions*
1 200-gram tin of chickpeas, rinsed and drained	**1** Combine all the ingredients in a food processor and blend together until smooth.
1 clove of garlic	**2** Check the consistency. If it's a little dry, add a drop more olive oil and blend again. Otherwise, spoon into a dish and enjoy.
1 tablespoon of lemon juice	
2 tablespoons of olive oil	
Small dash of Tabasco sauce	
Salt and pepper	
¼ cup of water	

Per serving: Calories 470 (From Fat 184); Fat 20.4g (Saturated 2.6g); Cholesterol Trace; Sodium 110mg; Carbohydrate 50.0g, Dietary Fibre 10.8g; Protein 21.5g.

Tzatziki

Tzatziki is a dip from Greece, served cool. Tzatziki is a bit runnier than hummus or guacamole, so it's more for dipping in fresh vegetables like strips of carrot or cucumber; something that won't go soft.

Preparation time: 5 minutes • **Cooking time:** Nil • **Serves:** 4

Ingredients	*Directions*
1 medium cucumber **250 grams thick Greek or natural yogurt** **Big pinch of chopped fresh dill or mint** **1 clove of garlic, crushed** **1 glug of olive oil** **Dash of Tabasco sauce** **Salt and pepper**	*1* Peel the skin off the cucumber with a vegetable peeler, chop the ends off and discard.
	2 Slice the cucumber in half lengthways and carefully scrape out the seeds with a small spoon.
	3 Finely chop or grate the cucumber into a bowl.
	4 Add the yogurt, herbs, garlic and olive oil to the cucumber. Add a dash of Tabasco to taste.
	5 Place the dish in the fridge to chill for an hour or two. Add the salt and pepper just before serving.

Per serving: *Calories 116 (From Fat 80); Fat 8.9g (Saturated 3.3g); Cholesterol trace; Sodium 133mg; Carbohydrate 5.0g, Dietary Fibre 0.7g; Protein 3.9g.*

Creamy Curry Dip

This dip has a spicy flavour to wake up your tastebuds. It goes great with some grilled naan or pitta bread cut into strips.

Preparation time: 5 minutes • **Cooking time:** Nil • **Serves:** 4

Ingredients	*Directions*
3 spoonfuls of mayonnaise	*1* Spoon the mayonnaise into a mixing bowl, add the korma sauce, mango chutney and yogurt and mix together.
1 spoonful of korma sauce (from a jar)	
1 spoonful of mango chutney	*2* Sprinkle the herbs over the top and serve.
2 spoonfuls of natural yogurt	
1 spoonful of fresh coriander or chives, chopped	

Per serving: Calories 101 (From Fat 87); Fat 9.7g (Saturated 1.8g); Cholesterol Trace; Sodium 108mg; Carbohydrate 2.9g, Dietary Fibre 0.2g; Protein 0.6g.

Tomato and Red Onion Salsa

Although some may disagree, I class salsa as a dip. After all, it tastes great and you can shovel the salsa into your mouth using a crisp.

Preparation time: 10 minutes • **Cooking time:** Nil • **Serves:** 4

Ingredients	*Directions*
5 or 6 tomatoes **1 small red onion** **½ to 1 fresh chilli**	*1* Cut the tomatoes in half and remove the seeds with a spoon. Chop the tomatoes into small pieces and place in a bowl.
Big pinch of chopped fresh coriander	*2* Peel and dice the red onion and add to the diced tomato.
1 teaspoon balsamic vinegar **1 clove of crushed garlic**	*3* Slice the chilli in half lengthways and remove the seeds. Finely chop the chilli and add half to the tomato.
Salt and pepper	*4* Add the coriander, vinegar and garlic and combine.
Pinch of sugar	*5* Season with salt and pepper and add a pinch of sugar. Taste the salsa and add more chilli if you want.
	6 Place into a serving dish, cover with cling film and chill in the fridge for a couple of hours to bring out the flavours.

Per serving: *Calories 29 (From Fat 3); Fat 0.3g (Saturated 0.1g); Cholesterol Trace; Sodium 45mg; Carbohydrate 5.5g, Dietary Fibre 1.3g; Protein 1.0g.*

Snacks for young and old alike

The best party food is stuff that's just as tasty eaten hot or cold. There's no point making an extravagant and delicious roast if your royal wedding plans involve a day-long celebration. Finger food is perfect for parties. It's easy to pick up and eat, and party-goers can mix and match it with the other food on the table.

Vegetable Samosas

You can buy pre-made samosas in the supermarket, but they're never as tasty as home-made ones. Plus, you can choose exactly what you want to put in your samosas and make them as spicy or as mild as you like.

Preparation time: 20 minutes • **Cooking time:** 20 minutes • **Makes:** 1 plate of samosas (about 15 to 20)

Ingredients	*Directions*
1 potato, peeled and quartered	**1** Preheat the oven to 200°C. Half fill a saucepan with water and bring to the boil. When hot, add a pinch of salt and the potatoes. Boil for 5 minutes and then drain. Don't worry about cooking them completely.
Oil (vegetable or groundnut)	
3 teaspoons of curry powder	
1 teaspoon of turmeric	
1 onion, peeled and finely chopped	
Small piece of ginger (about half the size of your thumb), peeled and finely chopped	**2** Run the potatoes under cold water and, when the potatoes are cool, cut them into pea-sized pieces.
½ cup of frozen peas	**3** Grab a frying pan and heat a drop of oil in the pan over a medium heat. When hot, stir in the curry powder and turmeric.
2 carrots, cut in half, then grated	
2 teaspoons of chilli powder	
Pinch of fresh, finely chopped coriander	
1 pack of filo pastry	
Saucer of melted butter	

4 When they've dissolved and are releasing a lovely, warming aroma (after about 30 seconds), chuck in the chopped onions and ginger and fry for about 5 minutes or until they turn brown. Now add the potato pieces and fry for another 5 minutes.

5 Add the peas and carrots and sprinkle the chilli powder and coriander over the mixture. Fry for about 3 minutes or until the peas defrost and then take the pan off the heat.

6 While that's cooling down, place 3 sheets of the filo pastry onto a clean chopping board. Brush or spoon a bit of the melted butter over each sheet, layer them on top of each other and then cut them into squares. They need to be about as big as a beer mat (about 5 centimetres by 5 centimetres).

7 Have a cup of water handy. Pop a teaspoon of the mixture from the frying pan into one corner of the filo square and fold the other corner over to cover it, making a triangle.

8 Dab your fingers in the cup of water and seal down the edge of the samosa. Place on a lightly oiled baking tray and brush with butter. Repeat this process until all the filling is used (you may need to use up to 9 sheets of filo pastry).

9 Repeat until the rest of the mixture and pastry is used up. Then place the baking tray of samosas in the oven for 10 to 15 minutes until they crisp up.

Per serving: *Calories 212 (From Fat 115); Fat 12.8g (Saturated 4.1g); Cholesterol Trace; Sodium 108mg; Carbohydrate 20.2g; Dietary Fibre 2.8g; Protein 4.1g.*

Mini Roast Beef and Yorkshire Puds

Honey, I shrunk the roast beef! Here's a classic British dish that gets miniaturised. Little Yorkshire puddings are filled with roast beef and horseradish sauce – Sunday dinner in the palm of your hand. They might even be eating these at the wedding reception!

You need a muffin tray for the Yorkshire puddings.

Preparation time: 10 minutes • **Cooking time:** 25 minutes • **Makes:** 1 plate of Mini Roast Beef and Yorkshire puds

Ingredients	*Directions*
2 eggs 100 grams of plain flour Pinch of salt 250 millilitres of milk	*1* Preheat the oven to 200°C. Crack the eggs into a large bowl and add the flour and salt. Add a drop of milk and whisk together. Keep adding the milk in and whisking until you get a light batter.
Chunk of butter	*2* Rub a little butter around each hole in the muffin tray to stop the Yorkshire puds sticking to the tray when they're cooked. Pour the batter into each hole in the muffin tray, filling it half full.
2 slices of cooked roast beef	*3* Place the tray in the oven and cook for 20 minutes.
Couple of spoonfuls of horseradish sauce	*4* Remove the tray from the oven and allow each pudding to cool on a wire rack.
	5 While they're cooling, slice the roast beef into squares small enough to place inside each Yorkshire pudding. Pop inside the Yorkshire puddings, top with a teaspoon of horseradish sauce and serve.

Per serving: Calories 107 (From Fat 50); Fat 5.5g (Saturated 2.8g); Cholesterol Trace; Sodium 84mg; Carbohydrate 9.5g; Dietary Fibre 0.4g; Protein 4.8.

Root Vegetable Crisps

These crisps go really nicely with some of the dips in earlier in the chapter.

Preparation time: 5 minutes • **Cooking time:** 10 minutes • **Makes:** 1 bowl of Root Vegetable Crisps

Ingredients	Directions
Selection of root vegetables (parsnips, sweet potato, beetroot, carrots)	*1* Peel and thinly slice the vegetables. The easiest way to do this is to use a vegetable peeler, but press a little harder as you're peeling so that you get a thicker peel.
	2 Pour about 3 centimetres of oil in a small saucepan and heat over a high heat.
Groundnut or vegetable oil	*3* While that's heating up, line a plate with some kitchen roll.
Salt	*4* After 2 minutes, drop a small bit of bread in the saucepan. If it quickly turns brown and crispy, the oil's hot enough, if not, keep heating the oil for a bit longer.
	5 Place a couple of the vegetables in the oil and fry until they turn brown and crispy (about 4 minutes). Then remove with a slotted spoon, drain off any excess oil and place on the kitchen roll to absorb any extra oil. Sprinkle with a little salt.
	6 Repeat until all the vegetables are used up. If the oil starts to spit, carefully take the pan off the heat and let it cool down slightly before moving it back on the heat and continuing. Add more oil if it becomes too shallow.
	7 Put all the vegetable crisps into a bowl and serve next to the dips.

Per serving: Calories 634 (From Fat 225); Fat 25.0g (Saturated 5.0g); Cholesterol Trace; Sodium 199mg; Carbohydrate 92.6g; Dietary Fibre 23.2g; Protein 9.6g.

Cheese and Ham Quiche

Face facts, a party isn't a party without a bit of quiche. And they're surprisingly easy to make.

Preparation time: 5 minutes • **Cooking time:** 40 minutes • **Makes:** 1 Cheese and Ham Quiche

Ingredients	*Directions*
300-gram packet of shortcrust pastry	*1* Preheat the oven to 200°C. Roll out the pastry until it's about half a centimetre thick and line the tin with it.
3 eggs	
240 millilitres of single cream	*2* Crack the eggs in a bowl and whisk until thoroughly mixed. When whisked, beat in the cream and add salt and pepper.
Salt and pepper	
2 slices of ham, cut into strips	*3* Place the ham and three-quarters of the cheese into the tin and pour the cream and egg mixture over the cheese and ham. Scatter the rest of the cheese over the top. Crimp (gently press) the edges of the pastry to make it look a little more quiche-like.
80 grams of grated cheese (Emmental cheese is very nice)	
	4 Pop in the oven for 40 minutes and allow to cool slightly before removing from the tin, slicing into portions and serving.

Variation: Cheese and ham is a pretty basic filling for quiches, so go ahead and try swapping the ham with spinach and tomato; cooked bacon and leek; fried mushrooms or smoked salmon.

Per serving: *Calories 358 (From Fat 245); Fat 27.2g (Saturated 10.6g); Cholesterol Trace; Sodium 216mg; Carbohydrate 17.6g; Dietary Fibre 0.6g; Protein 10.6g.*

Dinner Is Served

If you're opting for a sit-down affair (the Queen isn't; see the 'Royal wedding food facts' sidebar), here are a number of recipes. I include a soup and a number of starters, sides, and mains – plus a nice roast beef.

Royal wedding food facts

Food is always at the centre of great celebrations, and this year's royal wedding is no different. Here are a few tasty tidbits to tide you over:

✔ If you're opting for a buffet, you're in good company. Clarence House announced that wedding guests would enjoy a buffet-style spread after the 'I do's' instead of a formal lunch.

✔ If you can't bring yourself to cook or you fancy a pint after the party breaks up, you're in luck. Pubs will be permitted to extend their hours and serve alcohol until 1:00 a.m. on 29 and 30 April. A wedding present from the Government!

✔ If you're in the market for official commemorative plates or mugs for your dinner service, there's more good news: the Queen is holding the line on the VAT at her gift shops and not taking the 2.5 per cent increase that went into effect in January.

Butternut Squash Soup

This soup is a colourful, creamy and tasty starter.

Preparation time: 5 minutes • **Cooking time:** 20 minutes • **Serves:** 4

Ingredients	Directions
Glug of olive oil 1 onion, peeled and finely chopped 1 clove of garlic, peeled and chopped 1 large butternut squash, peeled and chopped into small cubes 1 litre of chicken stock	*1* Heat a drop of oil in a big saucepan over a medium to high heat and add the onions, garlic and sweet potato. Fry for five minutes until soft and starting to turn brown.
	2 Pour the stock into the saucepan, stir and turn the heat down to a medium setting. Leave to simmer for about 15 minutes, or until the squash has turned soft.
	3 Leave the saucepan to one side to cool down a bit, then pour the sauce into a blender and blend until smooth.

Per serving: Calories 154 (From Fat 11.0g); Fat 1.2g (Saturated 0.2g); Cholesterol Trace; Sodium 792mg; Carbohydrate 33.0g; Dietary Fibre 3.7g; Protein 2.8g.

Tomato and Mozzarella Bites

These classic Mediterranean morsels bring a bit of the continent to our grey shores at any time of the year and make a lovely starter.

Preparation time: 10 minutes • **Cooking time:** 5 minutes • **Serves:** 4

Ingredients	*Directions*
1 baguette, chopped into chunks	*1* Preheat the grill. Grill the pieces of bread until they're lightly browned (they won't take long).
3 cloves of garlic, peeled and chopped in half	
2 250-gram packets of mozzarella, sliced	*2* When the bread is toasted, take out from under the grill and gently rub the garlic clove halves over the toasted side.
Fresh basil (optional)	
3 tomatoes, sliced	*3* Top with a slice of mozzarella, then a basil leaf (if using), then a slice of tomato. Place on a plate. Repeat for all the other bites.
Olive oil	
Pepper	*4* When they're all on a plate, drizzle a bit of olive oil over them, grind pepper over them and serve.

Per serving: Calories 431 (From Fat 261); Fat 29.0g (Saturated 17.8g); Cholesterol Trace; Sodium 657mg; Carbohydrate 15.4g; Dietary Fibre 1.3g; Protein 27.1g.

Avocado Wrapped in Smoked Salmon

This is a quick starter that's delicious with a glass of white wine.

Preparation time: 20 minutes • **Cooking time:** Nil • **Serves:** 4

Ingredients	Directions
2 avocados	*1* Cut the salmon into strips about 1½ centimetres wide by 4 centimetres long.
2 fillets of smoked salmon	*2* Cut the avocado in half, separate the two halves and prise out the stone with a teaspoon.
1 lemon, cut in half (for juicing)	*3* Slice the skin away until you're left with the green flesh. Chop the flesh into cubes.
Pepper	*4* Roll the avocado cubes in the salmon strips and press a cocktail stick into them to hold them together. Repeat until you use up all the avocado and salmon.
	5 Squeeze the lemon over the bites, grind a little pepper over them and serve immediately.

Per serving: Calories 285 (From Fat 172); Fat 19.1g (Saturated 3.9g); Cholesterol Trace; Sodium 1885mg; Carbohydrate 1.4g; Dietary Fibre 2.6g; Protein 26.8g.

Salmon and Rocket Tagliatelle

This dish strikes the perfect balance: cool creaminess and tangy tart flavours.

Preparation time: 10 minutes • **Cooking time:** 35 minutes • **Serves:** 4

Ingredients	*Directions*
3 salmon fillets (about 5 centimetres square) **Handful of cherry tomatoes** **Salt**	*1* Turn the grill on to full power and, when hot, put the cherry tomatoes underneath the grill. Grill for 5 minutes, then add the salmon and continue grilling for another 5 to 10 minutes, until the salmon is cooked (the salmon should flake easily when pulled with a fork).
350 grams of tagliatelle (roughly 4 handfuls) **200-gram bag of rocket (torn into bite-sized portions)**	*2* Place the salmon and tomatoes to one side to cool down. While they're cooling, fill a large saucepan three-quarters full of water and put on the hob, full power, to bring to the boil. Add a pinch of salt and then the tagliatelle. Cook for about 10 minutes or until the pasta starts to soften.
4 spoonfuls of crème fraîche **4 teaspoons of capers** **Ground black pepper** **1 lemon, cut in half**	*3* When cooked, drain the tagliatelle through a colander and pour back into the empty pan. Break up the salmon with a fork (leaving the skin to one side) and put in the saucepan with the tagliatelle. Add in the rocket, crème fraîche, capers and grilled tomatoes, and stir well.
	4 Grind black pepper and squeeze some lemon juice over the pasta. Mix one final time and serve.

Per serving: *Calories 647 (From Fat 228); Fat 25.3g (Saturated 7.5g); Cholesterol Trace; Sodium 230mg; Carbohydrate 61.5g; Dietary Fibre 3.7g; Protein 43.4g.*

Warm Chicken Salad with Baby Spinach and Mozzarella

The spinach here is topped with succulent chicken breasts and crispy bacon. This salad is rather good with some warm crusty bread.

Preparation time: 15 minutes • **Cooking time:** 10 minutes • **Serves:** 2

Ingredients	Directions
For the dressing: **Olive oil** **Juice from ½ lemon** **Salt and pepper** **For the salad:** **½ an avocado** **Juice from ½ lemon** **3 slices of bacon** **2 chicken breasts, cut into 12 strips** **¼ red onion, peeled and finely sliced** **2 handfuls of baby spinach** **6 sun-dried tomatoes (optional)** **1 big ball of mozzarella** **Salt and pepper** **Olive oil**	*1* To make the dressing, mix 4 glugs of oil in a bowl with the lemon juice. Mix well and season with a little salt and pepper. *2* Preheat the grill to a medium setting. *3* Peel the avocado and then slice and place in a bowl. Squeeze over the other half of the lemon and mix carefully. (The lemon juice stops the avocado from turning brown.)

4 Place the bacon under the grill and cook until crispy, turning when necessary. Meanwhile, heat a frying pan with a drop of olive oil and gently fry the chicken strips until browned. Add the red onion slices and cook for a further minute.

5 Add the baby spinach and sun-dried tomatoes (if using) to the frying pan with the chicken and turn off the heat. Start stirring everything together; the spinach should start to wilt and shrink slightly. Break the mozzarella into bite-sized pieces and place in the pan. Season with a little salt and pepper.

6 Remove the bacon and place on a clean plastic chopping board. Carefully slice into strips.

7 Divide the chicken and spinach mixture between two plates, placing the avocado slices round the edge. Then place the bacon slices on top and drizzle over some dressing. Serve immediately.

Per serving: Calories 885 (From Fat 373); Fat 41.4g (Saturated 14.2g); Cholesterol Trace; Sodium 2356mg; Carbohydrate 36.8g; Dietary Fibre 9.9g; Protein 91.3g.

Beef Brisket with Newcastle Brown Ale Gravy

You braise this joint in a good old drop of Newcastle Brown Ale to give the meat a really nice flavour.

Preparation time: 10 minutes • **Cooking time:** 3 hours 30 minutes • **Serves:** 4

Ingredients	*Directions*
Oil (groundnut or vegetable, not olive oil) 1 kilogram of beef brisket 2 carrots, peeled and sliced 2 parsnips, peeled and sliced 1 onion, peeled and chopped 2 bottles of Newcastle Brown Ale Salt 2 baking potatoes, peeled and cut into pieces 2 teaspoons of cornflour	*1* Turn the oven to 180°C and place a roasting tin or casserole dish with fairly deep sides inside for five minutes to warm up.
	2 Heat a glug of oil in a large saucepan over a medium to high heat and add the beef brisket. Fry the brisket until each side has turned golden brown (4 to 5 minutes per side).
	3 Remove the casserole dish from the oven and place the carrots, parsnips and onion inside. Place the browned beef brisket (try saying that when you're drunk) on top of the vegetables.
	4 Pour over the Newcastle Brown Ale until the liquid fills about two-thirds of the roasting tin or casserole dish. Tightly cover with some kitchen foil and place in the oven for 30 minutes.
	5 After 30 minutes, turn the oven down to 140°C and cook for an hour.

6   After an hour, carefully remove the pan from the oven and uncover the foil. Carefully turn the beef over. Cover again with the tin foil and place back in the oven for another hour.

7   After an hour, fill a large saucepan three-quarters full of water and place on the hob to bring to the boil. When boiling, add a pinch of salt and add in the potato pieces. Cook the potatoes for 5 minutes.

8   Meanwhile, pour some oil on a baking tray and put it in the oven to heat up. When the potatoes have been boiling for 5 minutes, drain through a colander and carefully pour them onto the hot baking tray. Put them in the oven.

9   Remove the kitchen foil from the casserole dish and cook the uncovered beef and the potatoes for a final hour, bringing the cooking time up to 3 and a half hours.

10   Remove the beef from the pot and place on a clean chopping board (one you use for meat). Let that rest while you make the gravy.

11   Pour the liquid through a sieve into a saucepan, catching the vegetables in the sieve and put them onto warmed plates. Bring this liquid to the boil. Mix the cornflour with 3 teaspoons of cold water in a cup and pour into the juices to thicken it and make it into a gravy.

12   Remove the potatoes from the oven and place them onto the plates with the vegetables.

13   Slice the beef into layers and arrange on the plate with the vegetables. Pour the gravy into a jug and serve.

Per serving: *Calories 879 (From Fat 445); Fat 49.4g (Saturated 19.1g); Cholesterol Trace; Sodium 224mg; Carbohydrate 56.4g; Dietary Fibre 8.1g; Protein 52.2g.*

Chicken Wrapped in Parma Ham

This classic dish is still a firm favourite. The succulent chicken is wrapped in crispy Parma ham, and you can serve it with salad, fresh vegetables or whatever you fancy to be honest. Give this dish a try; it's dead easy.

Preparation time: 10 minutes • **Cooking time:** 20 minutes • **Serves:** 4

Ingredients	Directions
4 chicken breasts	**1** Preheat the oven to 180°C.
200 grams of mozzarella, sliced	**2** Place the chicken breasts on a clean chopping board (the one you use for meat) and slice each one open, almost cutting it in half.
8 slices of Parma ham	
Lemon juice	**3** Place a slice of mozzarella inside the cut chicken.
Black pepper	
	4 Wrap two slices of Parma ham around each chicken breast so that the ends meet underneath the chicken.
	5 Squeeze over some lemon juice and grind some pepper over each one.
	6 Place on a baking tray and put in the preheated oven for 25 to 30 minutes or until the chicken is cooked. (Check by pressing a knife in and making sure any juices run clear.)

Per serving: Calories 516 (From Fat 188); Fat 20.9g (Saturated 9.8g); Cholesterol Trace; Sodium 908mg; Carbohydrate 0.2g; Dietary Fibre Trace; Protein 81.7g.

Chapter 10

Delivering a Right Royal Pub Quiz

• •

In This Chapter

▶ Deciding where to hold your royal wedding quiz

▶ Forming the teams

▶ Selecting a format

▶ Divvying up the prizes

• •

*F*ingers on buzzers, here's the first question.

How many pub quizzes take place in the UK each week?

Answer: 22,445! That's a lot of questions but also a lot of fun.

In this chapter, I combine two great British traditions: pub culture and the royal family. As the festivities build up to the big day for Wills and Kate, why not organise a pub quiz for friends and family at the local boozer or at home?

But I know what you're thinking: a pub quiz takes a lot of organising, what with all those questions to compile, sheets to write up and answers to have ready to hand.

No fear, this chapter provides a ready-made pub quiz, divided up into ten rounds of ten brain-teasing questions, with multiple choice or simple true/false answers, so that you can strike a clever pose as the quizmaster if you so desire.

What's more, if you're a novice in the world of the great British pub quiz, I go through everything you need to know to organise a super shindig.

Sorting Out a Venue

A pub quiz doesn't have to be held in a pub – not a bit of it. Pub quizzes (or quiz nights) are held in church or community halls, theatres and schools across the country, often in aid of a good cause. In fact, many people who don't like a drink may prefer to go to a non-pub venue.

Here are a few things to check out before agreeing to book a venue:

- ✔ If you intend to sell alcohol (a good wheeze for raising extra money), check that the venue has an alcohol licence. Of course, pubs are fine but some community/church halls may be lacking one.

- ✔ Is the building up to date with its health and safety and fire regulations? Ask the venue's trustees or owners to show you the relevant certificates.

- ✔ Make sure that you aren't competing with another quiz night in the area. Call local pubs and halls to check; a finite number of people are into quizzes and you want to get maximum numbers!

Some halls and pubs ask for a deposit when booking the venue for your quiz night. So make sure that you do these checks thoroughly before handing over any cash as a deposit; and ask for a receipt!

Do your sums! Don't go booking a massive expensive venue if you're expecting just five teams. If you do, you're going to have to charge the teams a higher entry fee, which in turn puts off entrants.

Getting into Teams

You know the phrase that two heads are better than one – well, try four or five heads on for size! Most pub quizzes have an upper limit on the number of people who can sit on a single team – say five, six or seven – and the limit's for good reason.

A team with lots of members has a clear advantage in the brain compartment over teams of just one, two or three people. What's more, teams with lots of members tend to be a dull experience for those participants who strain to get their answers or ideas across to the team captain.

So at the outset let everyone know that a limit exists on the number of people in a team. If any big groups of people do want to play, ask them to split into two teams. And remember that more teams means a bigger prize pot and potentially more cash for the winners.

Ask each team to elect a team captain whose job is to collate the answers and hand them in at the end of each round to the quizmaster.

Each team needs a name, and so before kicking off the quiz, ask all the teams to decide on a name and as quizmaster write it on the top of each round's question sheet. Encourage the teams to come up with a royal or wedding-themed name.

Be firm with teams about timekeeping during the quiz. When collecting the papers or asking the team captains to bring them up to the front, don't start giving out the answers until the papers are collected in for marking. You don't want any dishonest souls to scribble down the answers you're giving out.

The idea of the quiz is for everyone to have a good time but don't forget the cold hard cash. Many quiz nights are organised in aid of a good cause and ask entrants to pay a small fee – normally a couple of pounds. Some of this amount is put into buying prizes and settling the venue hire cost (if necessary) and the rest goes to the good cause.

Formatting Your Pub Quiz

In the later section 'Royal Wedding Pub Quiz Questions', I provide 100 royal wedding questions for you to put to your quiz teams. By all means, draw up your own royal quiz questions as well, or mix and match some of my questions with your own. You can base more questions on the categories I use for the ten rounds or add new categories such as the following:

- ✔ Celebrities and the royals.

- ✔ Films connected with the royals.

- ✔ Religion and the royals.

- ✔ Eccentric royal behaviour and gaffes (contemporary and from the rich royal history).

> ✔ Science and the royals (may take some thinking about, but it's quite possible).

A quiz night isn't meant to be a re-run of school exams: it's supposed to be fun. If you're writing your own questions, throw in some fun questions and answers to make the room laugh. When you feel like it, add some bonus questions, too.

If by any chance you're a Cambridge Don of the quiz world, remember that not everyone has your encyclopedic knowledge. Therefore, toss in a fair percentage of easy questions for the teams. Nothing's more dispiriting than getting 'null point' – just ask the UK's Eurovision song contest entrants!

Spicing-up the scoring system: Introducing the joker

Here's an idea: give each team a joker to play on the round of its choice. When a team plays its joker in that round the members score double the points; this idea can help also-rans in the quiz with a massive scoring boost. In fact, a clever deployment of the joker can help one team to the pub quiz trophy.

Sharing the pain: Co-operative marking

Marking papers can be time-consuming and a bit of a pain – ask any secondary school teacher! So why not get the participant teams to mark each other's papers; for example, team A gets to mark team B's answers and vice versa.

Also, to save time you may want to give out answers and have marking done halfway through the number of rounds rather than after each and every round. However, check this arrangement out with the contestants first: keeping a running score adds tension and some people like to know how they're doing at the end of each round so that they can re-double their efforts on the next set of questions if they're trailing behind.

If planning a long quiz – such as the 100 questions and answers in this chapter – you may want to have a half-time break so that people can visit the toilet; or, most importantly, refresh their parched throats from the bar, perhaps with a royal-themed cocktail (a Chambord Royale or Royal Flush, anyone?).

Settling scoring disputes

People are naturally competitive and some people are *very* competitive. I've seen – and to my eternal shame been involved in – quite a few heated debates and disagreements at quiz nights. During one, I even saw fisticuffs among a neighbouring team – but I don't think that had anything to do with the quiz!

Such incidents are incredibly rare and most people enjoy the evening in the right spirit. Overwhelmingly disputes are settled in an instant and everyone gets on with having fun. But sometimes a dispute drags on and on. One point of conflict can be when the quizmaster gets teams to mark the scores. One team or individual may feel that a competitor team has been too harsh and marked their answers wrong when they should've been awarded a point.

If you, as quizmaster, become aware of this problem, take control and adjudicate who's right. Try to err on the side of generosity when deciding whether or not an answer is right or wrong.

Playing the End Game: Giving out the Prizes

A fun night has been had by all. The final round's papers have been collected, scores totted up, beers and wines consumed and now it's time for the big announcement of who wins what.

If you have lots of teams, you may want to award a first, second and third prize and even an extra special prize for the funniest or most ridiculous answer of the night.

Not everyone can win a prize but spreading the love a little is a good idea. Why not try awarding 'spot' prizes – a bottle of wine or a box of chocolates say – for answering a bonus question correctly. The beauty of the spot prize is that a team can be in last place and yet still win a prize just by answering one question correctly.

When selecting the prizes, provide items that the whole team can share, such as a case of wine or hamper of goodies. What's more, having a little trophy or certificate to acknowledge the winning team's success is always appreciated.

So let's get started!

Round One: Royal Family True or False

1. The Queen is notoriously careful with money and goes around Buckingham Palace turning off lights in rooms that aren't in use. She also has a fondness for keeping leftover food in Tupperware containers.

Answer: **True**

2. Prince Philip used to drive a black taxi cab around London when going on private appointments, but he would never pick up a fare.

Answer: **True**

3. Princess Beatrice is sixth in line to the throne.

Answer: **False** (she's fifth in line; her younger sister, Princess Eugenie, is sixth)

4. Anyone who's a Roman Catholic or marries a Roman Catholic can't ascend the British throne.

Answer: **True**

Optional bonus question: Which legal measure established this rule?

Answer: **Act of Settlement**

5. In a recent poll, 51 per cent of the British public said that they supported the retention of a constitutional monarchy.

Answer: **False** (regular support for the monarchy is in the high 70 per cent range)

6. The civil list – which pays the monarch a regular income from public funds – is set to be abolished in 2013.

Answer: **True**

7. The Queen's reign has been so long that 11 prime ministers have served her.

Answer: **False** (the number is 12: Churchill, Eden, Macmillan, Douglas-Home, Wilson, Heath, Callaghan, Thatcher, Major, Blair, Brown and Cameron)

8. The Queen owns 8 per cent of all the land in Canada.

Answer: **False** (she owns 89 per cent, but can't sell any of it because the Crown Land of Canada, as it's called, is held in trust for the nation of Canada and the Queen)

9. Prince Philip wrote the rule book for the sport of carriage driving.

Answer: **True**

10. The one-off charity game show *The Grand Knockout Tournament* (or *It's a Royal Knockout*) in which members of the royal family led teams of celebs and actors was broadcast 1997.

Answer: **False** (it was broadcast in 1987)

Optional bonus question: Name the four royals who took part in the show.

Answer: **Prince Edward, Princess Anne, Prince Andrew and Sarah Ferguson**

Round Two: Royals on the Box

1. Which female comedian co-wrote the BBC programme *The Royle Family*?

Answer: **Caroline Aherne**

2. The 'Royal Rumble' is a major annual event in which televised sport?

Answer: **Professional wrestling** (WWF is also acceptable)

3. Who was the Bond girl in the film *Casino Royale*, starring Daniel Craig?

Answer: **Eva Green played Vesper Lynd**

4. Which British character actress plays the matron in ITV's hospital drama *The Royal*?

Answer: **Wendy Craig**

Optional bonus question: What 1970s Carla Lane sitcom did this actress also appear in?

Answer: ***Butterflies***

5. Which member of the royal family was given a producer credit for the 2009 film *The Young Victoria*?

Answer: **Sarah Ferguson, Duchess of York**

6. Which journalist conducted the famous interview with Princess Diana when she said that three people had been in her marriage to Prince Charles?

Answer: **Martin Bashir**

7. Which London theatre hosted the 2010 annual *Royal Variety Performance*?

a) Palladium

b) Coliseum

c) Dominion

d) Prince Charles theatre

Answer: **a) London Palladium**

8. What time on Christmas day is the Queen's annual message broadcast?

Answer: **3 p.m.**

9. The 1999 BBC drama *All the King's Men* about the destruction of the Sandringham regiment during the First World War starred which famous British comedy actor in its lead role?

Answer: **David Jason**

10. Which suave actor played Jason King in the hit TV show of the same name?

Answer: **Peter Wyngarde**

Round Three: Royal History

1. The British national anthem is 'God save the Queen', which was first performed in 1745. What historical event coincided with this performance?

a) Defeat of the Spanish Armada

b) The Battle of Culloden and defeat of the Jacobite uprising

c) The Battle of Trafalgar

d) England winning the football world cup

Answer: **b) Battle of Culloden and defeat of the Jacobite uprising**

2. Which English king was killed at the battle of Bosworth Field in 1485?

a) Henry VII

b) Richard III

c) Henry V

d) Edward VII

Answer: **b) Richard III**

3. Queen Elizabeth II ascended the throne in 1952; who was her predecessor as monarch?

Answer: **George VI**

4. Queen Elizabeth II celebrates her Diamond Jubilee in 2012; who's the only other English monarch to celebrate 60 years on the throne?

a) George III

b) Queen Elizabeth I

c) Ethelred the Unready

d) Queen Victoria

Answer: **d) Queen Victoria**

5. The Queen married the Duke of Edinburgh in which year?

a) 1937

b) 1947

c) 1957

d) 1967

Answer: **b) 1947**

6. Which English king led his army to a crushing victory over the French at the Battle of Agincourt?

Answer: **Henry V**

7. Who was the first monarch to be both King of England and Scotland at the same time?

Answer: **King James I** (King James VI of Scotland is also acceptable)

8. Which Dutch prince seized the English throne in 1688, in what became known as the Glorious Revolution?

Answer: **William of Orange**

9. King Henry VIII was the father of Queen Elizabeth I and Mary I but he also had a son, Edward, who reigned for six years – which King Edward was he?

a) Edward IV

b) Edward V

c) Edward VI

d) Edward VII

Answer: **c) Edward VI**

10. Edward VIII is the only modern British monarch to have abdicated the throne; in which year did he do so?

a) 1906

b) 1916

c) 1926

d) 1936

Answer: **d) 1936**

Round Four: Royal Geography and Locations

1. The monarch is usually crowned in which building?

a) The House of Parliament

b) Buckingham Palace

c) Westminster Abbey

d) St Paul's Cathedral

Answer: **c) Westminster Abbey**

2. The Queen's official residence in Edinburgh is called what?

Answer: **Holyrood Palace** (Holyroodhouse is also acceptable)

3. The Balmoral estate is a favourite residence of the royal family. Approximately how many acres does the estate cover?

a) 6,400

b) 16,400

c) 64,000

d) 640,000

Answer: **64,000**

4. In which English county is the Sandringham estate?

Answer: **Norfolk**

5. The changing of the guard takes place at which royal palace during the summer months?

Answer: **Buckingham Palace**

6. What is the official London residence of Charles, the Prince of Wales?

Answer: **Clarence House**

7. In which year did Windsor Castle suffer a major fire?

a) 1972

b) 1982

c) 1992

d) 2002

Answer: **c) 1992**

8. Windsor Castle was originally built in 1070; which English monarch built it?

Answer: **William the Conqueror**

9. London contains several royal palaces: please name three.

Answer: **Any three from: Buckingham Palace, Hampton Court, Kew Palace, St James's, Westminster Palace and Kensington Palace**

10. Prince Charles has a keen interest in architecture; as part of that, he oversaw the development of a new town on some of his land. Name this experimental new town.

Answer: **Poundbury**

Round Five: The Royals and Sport

1. Which English premier league football club does Prince William support?

a) Manchester United

b) Chelsea

c) Aston Villa

d) Queens Park Rangers (QPR)

Answer: **Aston Villa**

2. Nine UK golf courses take turns to host the Open Championship. Five of these courses have 'Royal' in their name. Please name three.

Answer: **Royal St Georges, Royal Lytham & St Anne's, Royal Troon, Royal Birkdale and the Royal Liverpool Golf Club**

3. Which member of the royal family traditionally hands out the Men's Singles trophy at the Wimbledon tennis championship?

Answer: **Prince Edward, Duke of Kent** (in his role as president of the All England Tennis club)

4. The Queen Mother Champion Race is held at which UK racecourse?

Answer: **Cheltenham**

5. In the 1956 Grand National steeplechase, a horse owned by the Queen Mother famously half jumped and half collapsed in the home straight while leading the race. Name this horse.

Answer: **Devon Loch**

Optional bonus question: For an extra point, name the jockey riding the horse. Hint: he went on to be a famous novelist.

Answer: **Dick Francis**

6. The royal family is known to be enthusiastic about polo. How many players are on each side in a polo match?

Answer: **Four**

7. Which royal family member is the patron of the Scottish Rugby Union?

Answer: **Princess Anne**

8. Name the member of the royal family voted BBC Sports Personality of the Year in 2006.

Answer: **Zara Phillips**

9. The royal regatta at Henley on Thames is a highlight of the British sporting calendar. In which month is the regatta held?

Answer: **July**

10. The horse-racing meeting at Royal Ascot is also considered a major event in the British sporting calendar with the Queen in attendance. Traditionally, it's a five-day race meeting running from Tuesday to Saturday. Which of these days is known as Ladies' Day?

Answer: **Thursday**

Round Six: Royal Music

1. The Royal Philharmonic Orchestra was formed in which year?

a) 1846

b) 1906

c) 1946

d) 2006

Answer: **c) 1946**

2. Henry VIII is often credited, almost certainly wrongly, with having composed which famous musical piece?

Answer: **'Greensleeves'**

3. Prince Charles is a handy musician; which instrument does he play?

a) Cello

b) Violin

c) Trumpet

d) Triangle

Answer: **a) Cello**

4. How many number one singles have the rock band Queen had in the UK?

a) 6

b) 12

c) 18

d) 24

Answer: **c) 18**

5. 'God save the Queen' was a number one song by which band?

Answer: **The Sex Pistols**

Optional bonus question: In which year did 'God save the Queen' first make it to number one?

Answer: **1977**

6. The first line of the British national anthem is 'God save our gracious Queen'; what's the second line?

Answer: **'Long live our noble Queen'**

7. Edward Elgar's *Pomp and Circumstance* March No 1 is more popularly known as. . .

a) 'Land of Hope and Glory'

b) 'God save the Queen'

c) 'Rule Britannia'

d) 'Let it be'

Answer: **a) 'Land of Hope and Glory'**

8. The Royal Edinburgh Military Tattoo is a festival of marching and music that takes place throughout which month?

a) July

b) August

c) September

d) October

Answer: **b) August**

9. The wedding of Princes Charles and Lady Diana took place on 29 July 1981; what was the number one single in that week?

a) 'Don't you want me?' by The Human League

b) 'Do you really want to hurt me' by Culture Club

c) 'Billie Jean' by Michael Jackson

d) 'Ghost town' by The Specials

Answer: **d) 'Ghost town'**

10. Prince William and Kate Middleton became engaged on 16 November 2010; what was the number one single in that week?

a) 'Promise this' by Cheryl Cole

b) 'Only girl (in the world)' by Rihanna

c) 'Love you more' by JLS

d) 'Heroes' by the *X Factor* finalists

Answer: **b) 'Only girl (in the world)'**

Round Seven: Royal General Knowledge

1. Which member of the royal family is also a member of the Magic Circle?

Answer: **Prince Charles**

2. Which actress played the lead role in the film *The Queen*?

Answer: **Dame Helen Mirren**

Optional bonus question: Which actor played the youthful British prime minister Tony Blair in the same movie?

Answer: **Michael Sheen**

3. Which member of the royal family is considered a god by the inhabitants of the tiny south pacific island of Vanuatu?

a) The Queen

b) Prince Philip

c) Prince Charles

d) Prince Andrew

Answer: **b) Prince Philip**

4. Prince Andrew, the Duke of York served in the British military in the Falklands war; what was his role?

Answer: **Helicopter pilot**

Optional bonus question: Name the aircraft carrier he served upon.

Answer: *Invincible*

5. What was the name of the multi-million selling song, released for charity, which went to number one around the globe to commemorate the death of Diana, Princess of Wales?

Answer: **'Goodbye England's rose'**

6. At which university did Prince William and Kate Middleton study and meet?

Answer: **St Andrews**

7. At which famously rugged independent school was Prince Charles educated?

Answer: **Gordonstoun**

8. Which famous Latin phrase did the Queen use to describe the year 1992?

a) *Annus mirabilis*

b) *Annus horribilis*

c) *Annus terribilas*

d) *Annus bloodyawfulness*

Answer: **b)** *Annus horribills*

9. During the Thursday of Easter Week, the Queen distributes coins to elderly citizens. What is this ceremony called?

Answer: **Maundy Money** (Maundy Thursday is also acceptable)

10. The Queen is famously partial to which breed of dog?

Answer: **Welsh Corgis**

Round Eight: One's Commonwealth

1. Which Commonwealth country has the largest population?

Answer: **India**

2. Which city hosts the next Commonwealth games?

Answer: **Glasgow**

3. How many countries are members of the Commonwealth?

a) 34

b) 44

c) 54

d) 64

Answer: **d) 64**

4. In which city is the Commonwealth headquartered?

Answer: **London**

5. In 1977, the Commonwealth countries signed an agreement committing them to fighting apartheid; what was the name given to this agreement?

Answer: **Gleneagles Agreement**

Optional clue: The agreement was signed in a famous golf hotel, which was also the venue for the 2005 G7 summit of world leaders.

6. What is the name of the Commonwealth organisation that looks after the final resting place of up 1.7 million Commonwealth service personnel who fought in the 20th century's two world wars?

Answer: **The Commonwealth War Graves Commission**

7. What nation is currently suspended from the Commonwealth?

Answer: **Fiji** (suspended following a 2006 coup d'état). Note that Zimbabwe was suspended in 2002 but then withdrew from the Commonwealth in 2003.

8. In 1955, which major country secretly applied for membership of the Commonwealth but was turned down?

a) The United States

b) Spain

c) France

d) Germany

Answer: **France**

9. Who is the current head of the Commonwealth?

Answer: **Elizabeth II, Her Majesty the Queen**

10. The first formal meeting of the Commonwealth was held in 1944; which British prime minister presided over this first meeting?

Answer: **Sir Winston Churchill**

Round Nine: The Royals and the Arts

1. The Poet Laureate is appointed by the Queen. Name the current Poet Laureate.

Answer: **Carol Ann Duffy**

Optional clue: She's the first female Poet Laureate.

2. Which literary prize given annually is only open to writers from the Commonwealth as well as Ireland and Zimbabwe?

Answer: **The Man Booker Prize**

3. Which famous Soviet spy also held the role of Surveyor of the King's Pictures and in that role oversaw the Queen's Royal Collection of Art?

Answer: **Anthony Blunt**

4. Opened in 1871, which London concert venue can hold a maximum of 5,544 people, contains the second-largest organ in the UK and is topped by a huge wrought iron dome?

Answer: **The Royal Albert Hall**

5. The Royal Ballet School is based in Covent Garden in London. However, a junior Royal Ballet School also exists, for children under 11 to hone their skills; in which London park is this junior school located?

a) Hyde Park

b) Regents Park

c) Richmond Park

d) The Royal Car Park

Answer: **c) Richmond Park**

Optional bonus question: Which British blockbuster film about ballet featured this school?

Answer: ***Billy Elliot***

6. The Royal Academy was formed in 1768; which monarch was on the throne at the time?

Answer: **George III**

7. Which actor took the lead role in the Oscar-winning film *The Madness of King George*?

Answer: **Nigel Hawthorne**

8. In the early 1980s, which major London attraction's redevelopment did Prince Charles describe as 'a monstrous carbuncle on the face of a much loved and elegant friend'?

a) The British Museum

b) The National Gallery

c) The Tate Gallery

d) The Millennium Dome

Answer: **b) The National Gallery**

9. Which member of the royal family is reportedly a big fan of Canadian singer/songwriter Leonard Cohen?

Answer: **Prince Charles**

10. In which town is The Royal Shakespeare Company based?

Answer: **Stratford upon Avon**

Round Ten: The Royal Couple

1. In which African country did Prince William ask Kate to marry him?

Answer: **Kenya**

2. What subject did Kate Middleton study at University?

a) History of Art

b) English

c) Geography

d) Home Economics

Answer: **a) History of Art**

3. What type of stone was set in the middle of the royal engagement ring?

a) Ruby

b) Diamond

c) Emerald

d) Sapphire

Answer: **d) Sapphire**

Optional bonus question: What was the significance of this particular engagement ring?

Answer: **Prince Charles had given it to William's mother, Lady Diana**

166 Part III: Taking Part in the Festivities

4. Both William and Kate were the same age at the time of their engagement. How old were they?

Answer: **28**

5. Wills and Kate have said that they want to set up their home on an island off the coast of Britain. Which island have they chosen for their home?

a) Anglesey

b) Jersey

c) Wight

d) Tonga

Answer: **a) Anglesey**

6. What is Prince William's full-time job?

Answer: **He's a Royal Air Force search-and-rescue helicopter pilot**

7. The couple will marry at Westminster Abbey; name the last royal couple to marry at this venue.

Answer: **Prince Andrew to Sarah Ferguson in 1986**

8. On the day of their engagement, to which major news channel did William and Kate give a TV interview?

a) BBC

b) ITV

c) CNN

d) Sky

Answer: **b) ITV got the scoop of the year**

9. Between 2006 and 2007, Kate Middleton worked for which High Street retailer as a buyer?

a) Marks and Spencer

b) Primark

c) Jigsaw

d) Pound Land

Answer: **c) Jigsaw**

10. Name the other royal/commoner couple who became engaged at the end of 2010.

Answer: **Zara Phillips and Mike Tindall**

Part IV
The Part of Tens

The 5th Wave

By Rich Tennant

'What a wonderful swirled icing effect! How ever did you do it?'

In this part . . .

The Part of Tens is an essential part of any *For Dummies* book. These fun chapters contain ten websites about the royals and the big day, and ten royal homes.

Chapter 11

Ten Websites to Keep Up with the Wedding

*L*ast minute details are still to emerge about William and Kate's big day, so where can you catch up on all this info and differentiate between gossip and fact?

Britain is uniquely served by a host of great news websites able to bring you the latest royal wedding updates at the click of a mouse. What's more, cyberspace is buzzing with all things William and Kate with some fascinating royal wedding blogs to keep you informed and entertained.

Want to be able to keep up to speed with the latest developments in the wedding saga? This chapter outlines the best sites to check out, in no particular order.

BBC News Website

www.bbc.co.uk/news

The British Broadcasting Corporation (affectionately known as the Beeb or even Auntie Beeb) is the most important and respected state broadcaster in the world and serves its role as the place that Britons come to for news about major events at home and abroad. Its reputation for impartial, truthful reporting is second to none.

This excellence in journalism extends to the corporation's innovative news website. The Beeb has already broken a lot of royal wedding stories in advance of the big day and expect this to continue as 29 April nears.

On the day itself, the BBC is planning to stream TV coverage of the event on its website with interactive graphics, interviews with people in the crowd, and reader comments to keep you informed and entertained. The BBC News site is as close to a one-stop shop as you'll find for the royal wedding on the Internet.

The Daily and Sunday Telegraph

www.telegraph.co.uk

The *Daily* and *Sunday Telegraph* newspapers are traditionally seen as the most pro-monarchy within Britain's vibrant national newspaper sector. During their long courtship, stories and pictures of William and Kate often featured on the front pages of both newspapers as well as the website.

The royal wedding coverage both before the event and on the day itself is bound to be both extensive and informative. For many royal supporters, the Telegraph site is their first port of call for the latest on William and Kate's special day.

The Sun

www.thesun.co.uk

It's not all page three and football you know! *The Sun* prides itself on its royal coverage and getting the best scoops. However, their reporters can sometimes be viewed with suspicion after several run-ins with the royal family over the years. Nevertheless, expect *The Sun*'s website to go royal wedding barmy in the weeks and days before 29 April.

The Daily and Sunday Mirror

www.mirror.co.uk

The Sun's big rival, *The Mirror*, enjoys a better relationship with many of the royals and as a result tends to get more than its fair share of royal related scoops. *The Mirror*'s website has a special section entirely dedicated to the latest on the royal wedding as well as online reader polls and a Twitter feed from the newspaper's iconic gossipy 3 a.m. girls.

The Huffington Post

www.huffingtonpost.com

Proving the American fascination with all things royal, the Huffington Post – one of the most popular comedy, news and celeb sites stateside – produces almost daily royal wedding stories.

The Huffington Post's quirky take on the news is both irreverent and fun – just don't take it too seriously!

Some classics from the past on the royal wedding include the Queen's alleged dislike of wedding buffets – preferring a sit down meal – and that Kate Middleton shops at bargain clothes retailer TK Maxx (TJ Maxx in the States).

Hello Magazine

www.hellomagazine.com

Hello may not have exclusive rights to the pictures from the royal wedding, but that hasn't stopped the bestselling celeb magazine from going royal wedding mad. The magazine's site has a special section on the couple chock full of all the latest news as well as photo galleries galore from previous royal weddings and even some of Kate's old school photos – how embarrassing.

Readers are asked to vote on burning issues of the day such as which tiara Kate should wear on the big day and, of course, who should design the dress!

The site has a major focus on fashion and no doubt after the wedding Kate's dress will be emblazoned across your computer screen!

Sky News

www.skynews.com

The BBC's main news competitor, Sky, prides itself on breaking stories first, and this is certainly true of the royal wedding – one of the major stories of 2011.

Sky News was first to confirm the venue for the big day. If you're looking for up-to-date William and Kate news and any details of last-minute changes to the plans, definitely check out www.skynews.com.

Dummies.com

www.dummies.com

I may be a bit biased, but www.dummies.com is a great site at any time of the year. But in the weeks leading up to the wedding, it's even better. This site has videos featuring yours truly taking a tour of the various venues and viewing spots that are sure to feature on the wedding day.

The Royal Forums

www.theroyalforums.com

This site is about all things related to royalty in Britain and abroad. However, as the British royal family are the most high profile royals in the world, much of the information, posts and discussion threads on the site relate to our royal family, and the upcoming royal nuptials dominates.

This is the site for the real royal hobbyist. Want to know who is 999th in line to the throne or where all the royals were educated? You can find the answers here.

Marilyn's Royal Blog

www.marilynsroyalblog.blogspot.com

Marilyn Braun, the author of this blog, is fascinated by all things royal and the wedding and the couple are covered in great detail. From William's decision to give Kate his mother's engagement ring to the choice of official royal souvenirs, it's all there.

Readers can also access regular Royal Report podcasts through the site, and a lively chat room is a great place to discuss all things William and Kate.

Chapter 12

Ten Royal Newlywed Homes

In This Chapter

▶ Discovering the royal palaces

▶ Visiting the official residences

▶ Guessing where Wills and Kate may spend their Christmases

*N*ewlyweds need somewhere to live. Usually that means buying or renting a place with your new spouse or perhaps finding somewhere a bit bigger than where you live now.

Some young newlyweds aren't quite ready to make such a financial leap and may have to rely on mum and dad for shelter while they save hard for their first home. Whatever their situation, however, starting out on the journey of life together is always an exciting time for lovebirds.

Things are (how can I put it?) a bit *different* for Prince William and Catherine Middleton. They don't have to scan the estate agency windows or the small ads section of the local newspaper; they don't just have one or two places to choose from but ten. Yes ten!

The British monarch has several houses, and they're all large historic piles. One, Windsor Castle, has been in the family for around 1,000 years.

Several houses are *official residences*, buildings that go with the job and play a part in the work of the sovereign – holding receptions and banquets, for example, and housing the offices of key members of royal staff. Others are private houses that the monarch personally owns and are used by the royal family as family homes.

Many official residences are often open to the public, meaning that you can visit Windsor Castle, Buckingham Palace or the Palace of Holyroodhouse and see the settings of state banquets and royal rituals. The royal homes, such as Sandringham and Balmoral, contain exhibition rooms that are regularly open to the public.

Several of these palaces were built by royal family members for their spouses, although those days may well have gone.

In this chapter I look at ten royal residences in which Wills and Kate may live or maintain apartments, or at least visit for Christmas and holidays.

Buckingham Palace

This most famous royal house – the one on the 'must do' list for many tourists coming to the UK – is the sovereign's official London residence. Buckingham Palace became a royal home in 1761, when George III bought it for his wife Queen Charlotte (beats a pair of earrings!). At the time of the purchase, it was known as Buckingham House because it had been the London home of the Dukes of Buckingham.

George IV had the builders in and upgraded the palace in the 1820s, employing his favourite architect, John Nash, to double the size of the main block. Many of the state rooms date from this time. Another upgrade occurred during Victoria's reign, when more private rooms, such as nurseries, were added to accommodate the Queen's large family. Victoria also added the Ballroom, the palace's biggest room at nearly 37 metres (113 feet) long! The building's famous front, where red-uniformed soldiers stand on guard, dates from a still later remodelling from the time of George V.

When the Queen is in residence, the Royal Standard – a colourful flag with three lions emblazoned – flies from the flagpole atop Buckingham Palace. If there's no flag flying the Queen isn't in residence so you don't need to keep your camera lens trained on the balcony!

The Changing the Guard ceremony at Buckingham Palace is a big draw for tourists. The event is a kind of ritual handover when one group of guards departs and the next contingent takes over. After a certain amount of marching and music, the old guard skedaddles and the new one takes its place. The men who perform this ritual are from some of the most prestigious regiments in the British Army.

As well as hosting regular garden parties for members of the public who've performed good deeds for their fellow Britons, the Queen now opens the palace to the public at times during the summer months when the royal family isn't in residence.

Tourists can see the grand state rooms and marvel at the gilded furniture and the stunning paintings by the likes of Rembrandt, Rubens and Poussin. In addition, the Queen's Gallery – housing the vast royal art collection – is available for visitors to see. And if that's not enough, visitors can also look at part of the palace garden, a vast green oasis in the middle of London.

Buckingham Palace is also home to the Royal Mews, a large stable block that contains some extraordinary state vehicles such as the Gold State Coach (used for coronations) and the other coaches employed during important royal events. The limousines that the Queen uses on state occasions are also kept here. Some garage!

Wills and Kate are sure to maintain an apartment here.

Windsor Castle

Windsor Castle is the oldest royal residence and was originally built by William the Conqueror in the 11th century. Expanded, modified and made-over many times, the castle is now a fortress-palace and the largest occupied castle in the world.

Several monarchs contributed to making Windsor Castle the truly spectacular place it is today:

- ✔ Henry II rebuilt the large Round Tower and many of the castle walls in the 1170s.

- ✔ Edward III built the vast St George's Hall for the use of the Knights of the Garter.

- ✔ Edward IV and Henry VIII built the magnificent St George's Chapel in the 15th and 16th centuries.

- ✔ George IV, in the 1820s, rebuilt many of the state rooms and added the large Waterloo Chamber, designed to hold portraits of the characters involved in the defeat of the French emperor Napoleon at the Battle of Waterloo in 1815.

✔ Current Queen Elizabeth II had to restore nine main rooms and around 100 smaller rooms after the castle caught fire in 1992.

All that investment and involvement has made Windsor Castle a very special place. It's a favourite of the royal family – could this magnificent, ancient building provide a crashpad for Wills and Kate?

As well as being a much-loved family home, the castle is also the venue for all kinds of state occasions. St George's Hall, which is some 55 metres (around 170 feet) long, is a great room for big banquets – it houses a table that can seat 160 guests! Many foreign rulers, heads of state and dignitaries have enjoyed visits to Windsor.

St George's Chapel is one of the main attractions in the castle. This large, late-medieval building is stunning; its soaring windows and stone vault making it the equal of many cathedrals. It has been the scene of several royal weddings – but not for Wills and Kate (turn to Chapter 4 for more on their chosen location, Westminster Abbey).

St George's Chapel is the setting for the annual celebration of the Order of the Garter. The Queen, the Duke of Edinburgh, and their fellow Knights of the Garter process through Windsor Castle wearing the badge of the order, the Garter Star.

Visitors to Windsor Castle can also view some of the royal art collection as well as Queen Mary's Dolls' House, a perfect miniature designed by the major architect Edwin Lutyens.

The Palace of Holyroodhouse

The Palace of Holyroodhouse is the official royal residence in Scotland. The palace is at one end of Edinburgh's famous royal mile, the long street that connects Edinburgh Castle at one end with Holyroodhouse and the new Scottish Parliament building at the other. The Palace of Holyroodhouse is big, imposing and very Scottish – with its round towers and conical roofs, it looks like an even grander version of a Scottish baronial hall or tower house. Scottish kings and queens lived here before Scotland and England were united under one ruler in the 17th century.

The strange name, 'Holyroodhouse', comes from the palace's early history. The story goes that it was first founded as a monastery by David I in 1128. David had a vision of the cross, also known as the 'Holy Rood', and took it as a signal to found the monastery.

In the 16th century, James IV began the building next to the monastery, and a few decades later, this palace became the home of Mary, Queen of Scots. One of the most dramatic events of her reign, the murder of her secretary, Rizzio, took place in the Queen's apartments at Holyroodhouse.

Charles II made many improvements to the palace in the late 17th century, but for 200 years the royal family didn't use Holyroodhouse very much. But Queen Victoria, who loved Scotland, stayed here quite a lot on her way to and from her beloved Scottish country house, Balmoral.

The present Queen stays at Holyroodhouse quite regularly, especially at the end of June or in early July, when she usually spends a week in Edinburgh. This week sees a large garden party with some 8,000 guests and sometimes visits from world leaders.

Visitors to Holyroodhouse can see the state apartments, with their memories of Mary, Queen of Scots, their fine series of portraits of the kings of Scotland and some of the best tapestries in the world. The Queen's Gallery houses items from the royal collections.

Sandringham

Prince Albert Edward (the future King Edward VII) bought this country house in Norfolk in 1862. He rebuilt the house and estate completely, constructing new roads and cottages and re-landscaping the garden.

Sandringham became a much-loved family home and was the base for the shooting parties that were a favourite royal pastime.

During the time of Edward VII and George V, Sandringham clocks were moved on an extra half an hour during the winter so that the royals and their guests had more daylight hours for shooting. When people on the estate asked the time at midday, for example, the reply would be 12:30 ST – in other words 12:30 Sandringham Time.

Because it was bought privately, Sandringham is still held by the monarch as a private house – it doesn't belong to the nation but remains a favourite royal country retreat. Wills and Kate are sure to spend some relaxing times here and it's the house where the royals spend Christmas.

The estate includes the Sandringham Country Park, some 600 acres of woods and heathland, which is permanently open to the public. The Country Park's facilities include nature trails, caravan sites, a shop and a restaurant. At some times of the year, Sandringham House and its gardens and museum are open to the public.

Balmoral Castle

Prince Albert, Queen Victoria's beloved husband, bought the Balmoral estate in Aberdeenshire, Scotland, for her in the mid-19th century. The existing 15th-century castle was too small for Albert, Victoria and their family (after all, the couple had nine children), and so Albert quickly set about building a new castle. The building is very grand and very Scottish, with an impressive tower at one end. Like Sandringham, Balmoral is a private house of the monarch and isn't owned by the state.

The estate at Balmoral is enormous with some 50,000 acres in total, and the scenery, from mountain to moorland, is spectacular. Part of the estate is farmed, but not much good farmland exists because the royal land contains seven mountains that rise to more than 990 metres (some 3,000 feet) above sea level. Thousands of hectares are also given over to game resources, especially deer and grouse. Conservation is a high priority for the royal family, and measures are in place to protect the area's important wildlife (the bits that aren't shot of course!) and to plant native tree species.

The grounds, gardens and exhibitions of Balmoral Castle are open to the public for several months each year.

St James's Palace

Although not very well known, St James's Palace in central London is the sovereign's main, official residence. It was mainly built in the 1530s and was a royal home for some 300 years.

Henry VIII built St James's Palace, and quite a bit of his red-brick building survives. Later rulers added to the palace, producing the complex of buildings and courtyards that survives today. Visitors can see these only from the street, though, because St James's Palace isn't open to the public.

Foreign diplomats are always referred to as Ambassadors to the Court of St James, reflecting the fact that the palace is the sovereign's official residence.

The monarch doesn't live here anymore and the palace is now used for lots of different functions. For example, St James's is the London residence of the Princess Royal and Princess Alexandra. It also contains numerous offices of royal staff, housing the Royal Collection Department, the Yeomen of the Guard and the Queen's Watermen, among others.

Clarence House

Clarence House is in the middle of London near Pall Mall, right next to St James's Palace. The house was built in the 1820s and was first of all the home of Prince William Henry, Duke of Clarence, which is the origin of its name.

The Duke of Clarence eventually came to the throne as King William IV, and he continued to live there as king.

But Clarence House is well known today because, for nearly 50 years from 1953 until 2002, it was the home of one of the most popular members of the royal family: Queen Elizabeth the Queen Mother (grandmother to William and Harry). After the Queen Mother died in 2002, the house became the official residence of Price Charles, his sons and Charles's second wife, the Duchess of Cornwall.

The house accommodates offices for the staff of the Prince of Wales. As his residence, Clarence House is the last royal home in London to be used for the purpose for which it was originally designed.

Part of the building is open to the public during the summer months. The public rooms, where the Prince of Wales holds receptions and other events, are still largely furnished as they were in the time of the Queen Mother and contain pieces from her large collection, including numerous artworks by 20th-century British artists.

Kensington Palace

The royal family first had a palace on this site in west London when in 1689 William III bought a building called Nottingham House and employed the architect Christopher Wren to extend it. The result was Kensington Palace, and this elegant house was the favourite home of every ruler from William III until George II.

Kensington Palace is best known today because Diana, Princess of Wales made it her official home and had her office there. The palace now contains the London residences of a number of royal family members, notably the Duke and Duchess of Gloucester, the Duke and Duchess of Kent, and Prince and Princess Michael of Kent.

William and Harry spent much of their childhood at Kensington Palace as well, and the fond memories Wills holds has fuelled speculation that Kensington Palace will be the ultimate London residence of the happy couple. That is, of course, in a few years' time, after Wills' days as a helicopter pilot are finished.

The state apartments, together with a number of rooms housing royal exhibitions, are open to the public.

Highgrove House

The country home of the Prince of Wales is at Highgrove, near the small Cotswold town of Tetbury in Gloucestershire. Highgrove was built from 1796–98 and altered about 100 years later. The Prince's estate, the Duchy of Cornwall, bought the house in 1980. Charles was attracted to the house because its location in southwest England is near to many of the Duchy's other properties.

Since 1980, the Prince has altered the house, adding decorative touches to the exterior and making other changes, such as building a function suite in the grounds where he can hold meetings and other events.

But perhaps the biggest changes have been in the gardens. They have been redeveloped, with Prince Charles doing a lot of the planting himself. From the rose garden to the kitchen garden, Highgrove is now widely admired and famous worldwide.

Frogmore House

Frogmore is a little-known house near Windsor Castle on land that came into royal ownership during Henry VIII's time. Frogmore House itself was used by George III's wife, Charlotte, as a retreat away from London, and was also a favourite residence of George V and Queen Mary. Today, the elegant white house is occasionally used by the royal family for receptions and is open to the public on a few days each year.

Nearby is one of the great monuments of Victorian Britain, the Royal Mausoleum, built by Queen Victoria after the death of Prince Albert. When she died, her body was placed there beside her beloved husband's.

Life in Anglesey

It's befitting that the son of the Price of Wales will start his married life in Anglesey. Flight Lieutenant William Wales is based at RAF Valley on Anglesey, where he pilots a Sea King helicopter on search and rescue missions. Wills and Kate have lived on the island for about a year and expect to continue on for another two years. When on duty, William lives in quarters, but he and his new wife will certainly be house hunting in the coming months. The happy couple are said to enjoy life on Anglesey where the paps are at a minimum, and they're able to pop into their local with minimal fuss.

Index

Notes

Notes

Notes

Notes

Best of British!

978-0-470-68637-9

978-0-470-97819-1

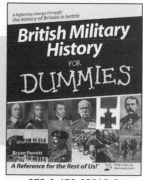

978-0-470-03213-8

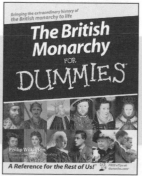

978-0-470-05681-3

Available wherever books are sold.

FOR DUMMIES

Making Everything Easier!™

UK editions

BUSINESS

Marketing Kit FOR DUMMIES

978-0-470-74490-1

Business Plans Kit FOR DUMMIES

978-0-470-74381-2

Project Management FOR DUMMIES

978-0-470-71119-4

SELF-HELP

Cognitive Behavioural Therapy FOR DUMMIES

978-0-470-66541-1

Neuro-linguistic Programming FOR DUMMIES

978-0-470-66543-5

Mindfulness FOR DUMMIES

978-0-470-66086-7

HOBBIES

Growing Your Own Fruit & Veg FOR DUMMIES

978-0-470-69960-7

Allotment Gardening FOR DUMMIES

978-0-470-68641-6

Electronics FOR DUMMIES

978-0-470-68178-7

Available wherever books are sold.

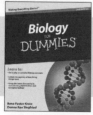

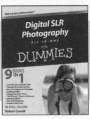

Internet

Blogging For
Dummies, 3rd Edition
978-0-470-61996-4

eBay For Dummies,
6th Edition
978-0-470-49741-8

Facebook For
Dummies, 3rd Edition
978-0-470-87804-0

Web Marketing
For Dummies,
2nd Edition
978-0-470-37181-7

WordPress
For Dummies,
3rd Edition
978-0-470-59274-8

Language & Foreign Language

French For Dummies
978-0-7645-5193-2

Italian Phrases
For Dummies
978-0-7645-7203-6

Spanish For
Dummies, 2nd Edition
978-0-470-87855-2

Spanish For
Dummies, Audio Set
978-0-470-09585-0

Math & Science

Algebra I For
Dummies, 2nd Edition
978-0-470-55964-2

Biology
For Dummies,
2nd Edition
978-0-470-59875-7

Calculus For
Dummies
978-0-7645-2498-1

Chemistry For
Dummies
978-0-7645-5430-8

Microsoft Office

Excel 2010 For
Dummies
978-0-470-48953-6

Office 2010 All-in-One
For Dummies
978-0-470-49748-7

Office 2010 For
Dummies,
Book + DVD Bundle
978-0-470-62698-6

Word 2010 For
Dummies
978-0-470-48772-3

Music

Guitar For Dummies,
2nd Edition
978-0-7645-9904-0

iPod & iTunes
For Dummies,
8th Edition
978-0-470-87871-2

Piano Exercises
For Dummies
978-0-470-38765-8

Parenting & Education

Parenting For
Dummies, 2nd Edition
978-0-7645-5418-6

Type 1 Diabetes
For Dummies
978-0-470-17811-9

Pets

Cats For Dummies,
2nd Edition
978-0-7645-5275-5

Dog Training For
Dummies, 3rd Edition
978-0-470-60029-0

Puppies For
Dummies, 2nd Edition
978-0-470-03717-1

Religion & Inspiration

The Bible For
Dummies
978-0-7645-5296-0

Catholicism For
Dummies
978-0-7645-5391-2

Women in the Bible
For Dummies
978-0-7645-8475-6

Self-Help & Relationship

Anger Management
For Dummies
978-0-470-03715-7

Overcoming Anxiety
For Dummies,
2nd Edition
978-0-470-57441-6

Sports

Baseball For
Dummies, 3rd Edition
978-0-7645-7537-2

Basketball For
Dummies, 2nd Edition
978-0-7645-5248-9

Golf For Dummies,
3rd Edition
978-0-471-76871-5

Web Development

Web Design All-in-
One For Dummies
978-0-470-41796-6

Web Sites
Do-It-Yourself
For Dummies,
2nd Edition
978-0-470-56520-9

Windows 7

Windows 7
For Dummies
978-0-470-49743-2

Windows 7 For
Dummies, Book + DVD
Bundle
978-0-470-52398-8

Windows 7 All-in-One
For Dummies
978-0-470-48763-1

Available wherever books are sold. For more information or to order direct: U.S. customers
visit www.dummies.com or call 1-877-762-2974. U.K. customers visit www.wileyeurope.com
or call (0) 1243 843291. Canadian customers visit www.wiley.ca or call 1-800-567-4797.